THE CLARENDON BIOGRAPHIES

General Editors: C. L. MOWAT and M. R. PRICE

SUN YAT-SEN

by

R. Bruce

OXFORD UNIVERSITY PRESS

1969

Oxford University Press, Ely House, London W.1

GLASGOW NEW YORK TORONTO MELBOURNE WELLINGTON
CAPE TOWN SALISBURY IBADAN NAIROBI LUSAKA ADDIS ABABA
BOMBAY CALCUTTA MADRAS KARACHI LAHORE DACCA
KUALA LUMPUR SINGAPORE HONG KONG TOKYO

Printed in Great Britain by Richard Clay (The Chaucer Press), Ltd.,
Bungay, Suffolk

CONTENTS

LIST OF PLATES

1

BOYHOOD AND YOUTH

SUN YAT-SEN, the founder of the Chinese Republic, was born on 12 November 1866 at Choyhang, a village in the extreme south of China. His father was a farmer, a man of some standing in the village, for his house was larger than most and he was able to employ one or two labourers in his scattered rice fields.

Choyhang was like thousands of other villages in southern China. Its grey-brick, single-storey buildings were crowded together along narrow, open-drained streets with no wheeled traffic. Goods were carried on shoulder-poles and few 'horse roads' linked the villages of China in the nineteenth century. Pigs, hens, and water-buffaloes walked the narrow alleys along with the people. The most prominent building was the two-storey pawn-shop which served as a bank and a store for valuables such as padded winter gowns during the long, hot months of summer. There was a temple for the worship of ancestors which was also the village school and another temple containing the figures of gods and idols, relics of a long-since decadent Buddhism. A wall surrounded the village for protection against thieves and river pirates.

Sun's birthplace was in sub-tropical Kwangtung, the most southerly of China's maritime provinces. Some eighty miles from the provincial capital, Canton, the village stood among low mountains in the district of Hsiang Shan ('Fragrant Mountains') on the western shore of the Pearl River estuary. It was quite near the Portuguese colony of Macao and fifty miles across the delta from Hong Kong. Villages in Kwangtung, by Chinese standards, were wealthy. They suffered no disasters of flood or drought like those on the plains of north China more than a thousand miles away. But by Western standards life in Choyhang was simple, almost primitive and it had changed little for centuries.

There were six children in the Sun family, three boys and three girls, but a boy and a girl died at an early age. Yat-sen was the fifth child. These two words mean 'leisurely' and 'saintly'. The surname, Sun, not one of the commonest, means 'grandson' or 'descendant'. Sun Yat-sen had a number of given names, for in his day it was common to be given one at birth, another on going to school, and another on coming of age. Chinese given names usually indicate a quality or virtue or have a literary allusion. Among Chinese Sun Yat-sen is usually known as Sun Wen, 'wen' meaning 'literature' or 'scholarship', or Sun Chung-shan meaning 'middle mountain'.

The Sun family was highly respectable, conservative, and ordinary. Sun Tat-shing, the father, was a thin, ascetic man with a reputation for honesty. As a young man he had worked for a time as a tailor in Macao and returned to the village with enough cash to rent a few fields in addition to those he owned. At the late age of thirty-three he married a girl of eighteen of the surname Yeong from a neighbouring village. She was a plain woman with strong, pleasant features, a broad nose and heavy chin, but it was a face of character. Like her husband she was conservative, observed the rites to the Sun ancestors, and taught her children the virtues of filial piety. Her feet were bound so that she hobbled about the house with difficulty. The constricting of the feet in childhood was regarded as necessary for the gentility and elegance of Chinese ladies. Mrs. Sun could read and write, a rare achievement among women, especially farmers' wives.

Sun Yat-sen was more like his mother than his father. He was short but strongly built, his face broad, his eyes widely set, and his forehead high. His firm chin and mouth showed a strong, stubborn character. Like his father and elder brother, he wore his hair long in a pig-tail or queue. At the age of eight he went to the village school, but his father required him to work in the fields after school and all day during the harvest. Even as a boy he was a rebel. It is recounted that he fought bigger boys who were behaving like bullies. At the age of ten he protested at the practice of foot-binding, particularly in the case of his own sisters. He stood up to thieves who had broken into the house of a rich neighbour, and he rebelled against the teaching methods of the schoolmaster.

Rich men and Mandarins (magistrates and other high officials) employed tutors for the education of their children. Ordinary people sent their boys, and occasionally their daughters, to the school in the ancestral temple. But for the majority in China there was no schooling at all.

Yat-sen was the brightest boy in the school at Choyhang. He was diligent and learned quickly. Study consisted of learning the infinitely complicated system of writing and through this the wisdom of the Chinese tradition. Thousands of symbols or characters (one for each word) had to be learned by rote and long passages from the Classics committed to memory. The pupils chanted in unison or recited singly, face to the wall, from the Confucian Classics. There were the Great Learning, the Analects, and the Book of Mencius. A simpler text was the Three Character Classic, but they were all profound, obscure, and far beyond the understanding of peasant children or indeed of any children.

Yat-sen protested. He told the schoolmaster that memorizing was no use without understanding. He was bored and angry. The teacher was astounded. A boy should never challenge a teacher and it was impudent to claim to understand the great writings. For one thing, it was almost certain that the teacher did not understand any more than his pupils. Yat-sen escaped chastisement by accepting the situation and continued to excel in learning characters and memorizing the Classics.

In these dull lessons lay much of the culture of China. They were passages from the Confucian books of the first millennium B.C., the foundation of a very great civilization. Confucius, China's most famous philosopher, saw in the family the basis of society. He laid down rules of conduct for children and parents and for all members of society. He defined the virtues of the ideal Ruler, the Son of Heaven. Loyalty to parents and all superiors was extolled. The ancestors must be revered. Rites and ceremonies are important, for men need conventions to bind them to good ways. The superior man should always act with decorum, should be self-controlled, and careful of every word and action. Dignity and scholarship, propriety, loyalty, and filial submission were the supreme virtues.

As for God and man's relations with him, Confucian doctrine was less categorical than most religious systems. There was the impersonal notion of Heaven or T'ien and the more human concept of Shang Ti, the Ancestor Above; but for the ordinary people the spirits of their own ancestors were the most important beings in the world beyond man's society and beyond the grave. Only the Emperor need make ritual offerings to T'ien or Shang Ti, for he was himself of celestial origin as were his ancestors. He was T'ien Tzu, the Son of Heaven. Confucius was much concerned with man's political and social relations, for these seemed to him to have priority over supernatural matters.

In Sun Yat-sen's childhood the Confucian code still prevailed in Choyhang and throughout the Chinese Empire. But other ideas were spreading. For the first time it was coming to be realized that there were other civilized ways of living outside the great Confucian tradition.

When he was a very small boy Sun Yat-sen listened to stories of the West Men told by his grandmother. They sailed up the Pearl River in ships driven by steam. Their skins were pale, their eyes blue, and they grew thick beards. They ate with knives and had no decorum. Yat-sen was fascinated. Very soon he was to learn a great deal more about these West Men.

Two widowed aunts lived in the Sun household. Their husbands had been Mr. Sun's brothers, who had sailed for America to seek their fortune in the Gold Rush of 1849. One died at sea, the other reached California but was never heard of again. Without prospect of other husbands the two widows found refuge with their brother-in-law in the house at Choyhang. Yat-sen's elder brother Tak-cheong followed the example of his uncles and sailed for Honolulu when he was eighteen. Yat-sen was only six at the time.

Tak-cheong was one of many Chinese who went to Hawaii at this time. Mostly from his own province of Kwangtung they were peasants and labourers who soon established themselves as

farmers and traders. Tak-cheong, or Ah Mei—'Eyebrows'—
to use his family name, was quickly successful. On a small piece
of land near the modern Pearl Harbour he grew rice and sugar
cane and opened a small store to sell food and farm equipment
to his fellow-countrymen. In six years he had earned enough to
sail home to Choyhang to marry a wife of his parents' choosing
and bring back with him goods and money in such quantity
that he was the envy of the village. His greatest admirer was
Yat-sen, now eleven. The boy pleaded with his father to let him
go back with Ah Mei who was eager to have him as a helper,
but Sun Tat-shing refused. It was enough that his two brothers
should have died and his eldest son should leave home.

The official Chinese attitude to emigration was hostile. According to the Confucian code a good son did not leave his parents
and only an eccentric would wish to leave the culture of China
for the darkness of barbarian countries. These ideas had little
effect in the maritime provinces of the south. There was practically no migration from the interior, least of all from the conservative north near the Imperial capital, Peking. But the south
was the gateway to the outside world. It had been made so by
Imperial edict. International trade was disliked and discouraged.
Throughout the eighteenth century and the first half of the
nineteenth foreign trade was allowed at only one port, Canton.
It was not surprising, therefore, that it was the Chinese on the
south coast who went abroad to seize the opportunities of an
expanding commerce.

In 1879, the year after Ah Mei's return to the village, Sun
Yat-sen sailed for Honolulu. He was not yet thirteen. Ah Mei
wanted him to help in the shop, the boy was clamouring to go
and at last his father yielded. The steamship which carried him
from Hong Kong fascinated him. The power of her engines and
the orderly skill of the voyage excited him even more than the
appearance of the tall, bearded British sailors. He had no fear,
only boundless curiosity and excitement, and although he was
unaware of it this voyage was Sun Yat-sen's first step on the
revolutionary road.

Looking after Ah Mei's shop at Ewa, the village near Honolulu, bored Yat-sen. He saw Americans and British around him as well as Chinese planters, Hawaiians, and Japanese. He saw a new world and he wanted to learn more about it. He asked Ah Mei if he could go to school. With reluctance the elder brother agreed and Yat-sen entered the Church of England boarding-school at Iolani at the age of thirteen. The headmaster, Bishop Willis, and the English teachers admired the boy's diligence and good manners. When he went to the school Yat-sen knew practically no English, but within a year he was winning prizes in English grammar. Yat-sen was among the first of his people to have a foreign education. Its influence was profound.

He studied geography, mathematics, and science. He studied the Bible. Prayers, chapel services, psalms, and recitations from the New Testament took the place of the Confucian Classics. Yat-sen did not rebel against the discipline of this school; he loved it. After more than two years there he decided to become a Christian. It is not clear whether or not he was baptized but it is certain that he was then, at the age of fifteen, an enthusiastic admirer of Western ways and the Christian religion. This was too much for Ah Mei. Along with his remittances of money to the family at home he sent reports of increasing concern about his brother's adherence to Western ideas. It was decided to send him back before it was too late. After more than three years in Hawaii Yat-sen returned to Choyhang village at the age of sixteen.

His father was getting old and infirm, but the family was not in difficulties because Ah Mei's generous and regular gifts kept them wealthy by village standards. Yat-sen helped with farming and household affairs but he was discontented, for he despised the old ways, the inefficiency and the corruption of officials. A few months after his return his rebellious discontent caused a scandal which gravely embarrassed his parents and led to his final departure from Choyhang.

The Chinese year was marked by rites and festivals—the spring sweeping of the graves, the Dragon Boat races, the autumn harvest, and, greatest of all, the New Year, the national birthday. These occasions Yat-sen regarded with indifference but not hostility. But the worship of wooden gods and idols was too much for him. One day he went with a group of youths to the Temple of the North God where people had been offering gifts and burning incense to the idols. In a rage Yat-sen walked up to the figures and called upon the villagers to give up their superstitions. He reached up to a gaudily coloured idol and broke off a part of its arm to show that it could be denounced with impunity.

The worshippers were shocked and terrified by this sacrilege. They ran from the temple to tell the village elders and all the people what had happened. There were some who shared Yat-sen's scepticism, but to the majority it was a disgraceful act. To save more embarrassment and gossip Mr. Sun decided to send his son away from the village. To his relief and advantage Yat-sen was sent to Hong Kong to attend another Christian school.

With help from Ah Mei he first went to the Diocesan School and then to Queen's College. Again he was in a Christian environment and this time his baptism into the faith is recorded. It was in the spring of 1884 that he went to Queen's College. Only a month or two later he was called back to the village to get married. He was not yet eighteen, a Christian and a rebel against the old customs, and yet he submitted to marrying a girl chosen by his father and mother, a girl of the Lo family from his own village. But Yat-sen was always loyal to that central part of the Confucian doctrine—filial piety, the submission of a son to the will of his father. What is more, many years were to pass before choice could be exercised in marriage. Courtship was unknown. Finding a wife or a husband for their children was the business of parents assisted by astrologers and a professional go-between.

The girl chosen for Sun Yat-sen was typical of her peasant society. She was comely and pleasant, not in any way striking. She had had very little education, had a calm and peaceful disposition, well suited to the custom which required women to lead a life of obedience—obedience to their fathers before marriage, to their husbands, and to their eldest son on widowhood. The young Miss Lo was no rebel like her husband. Although it was a marriage which suited the interests of the Sun and Lo families in

Choyhang and the horoscope of the astrologer more than the
wishes of the young man, Yat-sen was fond of his wife, though as
a wandering revolutionary he was to spend little time with her.
From this marriage came three children, two daughters and a
son—Sun Fo, later to be a leading figure in the government of
Chiang Kai-shek.

In the autumn of 1884 he paid a visit to Hawaii at the invita-
tion (and expense) of Ah Mei. It was a business meeting to dis-
cuss the family fortunes. Ah Mei expressed his concern over
Yat-sen's Western thought and his belief in Christianity, but no
crisis occurred and the younger brother went back to Queen's
College.

In 1884 France went to war with China over Annam, part of
the country now called Vietnam. For many centuries Tongkin
in the northern part of the country had been either part of the
Chinese Empire or a feudatory of China. The extension of
French power northward towards the Chinese provinces of
Yunnan and Kwangsi brought her into conflict with China and
war ensued. By 1885 China had been roundly defeated. Sun Yat-
sen, the Christian schoolboy, was shocked and ashamed at his
country's weakness. He began to think politically, but it was not
until he became a medical student two years later that Sun Yat-
sen, the political revolutionary, began to emerge.

After leaving Queen's College in 1886 at the age of nineteen
Sun Yat-sen went to Canton and began to study medicine. The
Pok Tsai Hospital, an Anglo-American missionary establishment,
had just been opened under the direction of a fiery, white-bearded
Scotsman, Dr. John Kerr. Here again was Christian influence.
He returned to Hong Kong in 1887 and entered the newly opened
Medical School for Chinese Students.

The Medical School was largely the creation of Sir Patrick
Manson, the founder of tropical medicine, and of a Chinese doctor
named Ho Kai, a graduate of Aberdeen, who was later knighted
for his public work. Manson retired soon after he had set up the
school and was succeeded as Dean by Dr. James Cantlie. Sun
Yat-sen was one of the very first students, and he was a success
from the beginning. Cantlie said of him later: 'Sun studied

medicine as he has studied everything else, ardently.' But his activities were by no means confined to medical studies.

He became a remarkably social person. He had many friends and loved talking to all hours of the night. He entertained generously, inviting students to tea-houses or to his lodgings for dinner. All his money came from Ah Mei. Sometimes he got into debt because of his generous habits and complete unconcern for money. But as soon as the next remittance came from Honolulu he paid his creditors. He despised misers.

Yat-sen enjoyed his studies. Early each morning he climbed the steep hill to the Alice Memorial Hospital (named after Dr. Ho Kai's English wife) well before the appointed time. Dressed in a long gown, a round skull-cap on his head, and his well-plaited pig-tail reaching below his shoulders, the young medical student applied himself with such zest and industry that he became Cantlie's favourite pupil. At this stage Sun saw in modern medicine one solution to China's backwardness. Modern medicine could not only cure diseases, it was also a symbol of scientific method and application in which his country was desperately backward. But he was soon to find that his real calling was politics, not medicine.

There were three other students of medicine who were his particular friends. Every subject was their talking point but most of all China, China in defeat and decline. They became known as the Four Bandits and Sun was their leader. He acquired some notoriety. Once, when he seemed overconfident and almost arrogant, a friend asked him: 'Do you want to become the Governor of Kwangtung?' 'No,' said Sun. 'Or the Emperor's Chief Commissioner?' 'Not that either,' was the reply. 'Well, then, you want to be the Emperor himself?' 'No,' said Sun with quiet confidence. 'I want to overthrow the Manchu Emperor and have China governed again by the Chinese.' It was nearly twenty-five years later that Dr. Sun Yat-sen witnessed the downfall of the Manchu Empire and became the first President of the Republic of China.

2

CHINA IN THE NINETEENTH CENTURY

THE nineteenth century for China was the period of her greatest decline. It was not only a time of political weakness and corruption such as had marked the end of dying dynasties in the past. It was the first time in her long history that she was confronted by a civilization more powerful than her own. In the past, dynasties were replaced when the Emperor became incompetent and rebellion brought new and vigorous leaders to the Dragon Throne. Sometimes the dynasty was overthrown by a foreign invader. But in each case there was no question as to the continued existence of the Confucian Empire, merely a change in the family in power. The fabric of Chinese culture remained intact. In the nineteenth century, however, the fall of the dynasty saw the fall of China herself.

For more than two thousand years China had been supreme in East Asia. The source of culture and political power, the Chinese Empire at times extended deep into central Asia. During the Han Dynasty, in the second century before Christ, her armies and emissaries pushed so far west that they were in vague contact with Rome. In the T'ang Dynasty (A.D. 618–906) China's imperial power reached the frontiers of India and even in the Ch'ing Dynasty (1644–1911) her influence again stretched to the Himalayas. China had been the Greece and the Rome of East Asia, but her hegemony had been much longer. Not even Japan, the most successful of her cultural offspring, could challenge China's leadership until the close of the nineteenth century. To humanist Europe of the eighteenth century the civilization of China presented a picture of ordered harmony, scholarship, and good taste, and the great houses of France and England were adorned with things Chinese.

China's last dynasty was a foreign one. It had been established in 1644 by the invading Manchus, 'barbarian' tribes who lived to the north of the Great Wall. The Manchu kings called their house the Ch'ing, the 'Brilliant' Dynasty. They rapidly acquired Chinese culture and encouraged Chinese scholarship. Having none of their own, this was in their interest as it secured the allegiance of the Confucian scholars who administered the country. Without the support of the scholars they could not have ruled the enormous country which they had taken over. For the first forty years after they had established their capital at Peking (not far from their ancestral home in the north) the Manchus controlled only the northern half of China. In the south they faced resistance, rebellion, and hatred.

Although the Manchus zealously promoted Chinese culture and in the eighteenth century secured peace at home and a great empire to the west, they never obtained the loyal support of the southern Chinese. In the great Confucian tradition the civil service was recruited by competitive examination in the Classics. Half the posts were reserved for Manchus and the other half were given mainly to northern Chinese. The southern scholars were distrusted. Much of the wealth came from the central and southern provinces but the imperial revenue was largely spent in Peking and the surrounding area. It is not surprising that rebellions to remove the Manchus and restore the Ming house were southern enterprises.

Although foreign in race and origin the Manchu rulers became more Chinese than the Chinese themselves. Their zeal for Chinese culture was unbounded. Under Imperial patronage new commentaries on the Classics were published; poetry, painting, and calligraphy were practised at the Court and in the reign of the great Emperor K'ang Hsi a vast dictionary was compiled. The middle period of the Ch'ing Dynasty (the eighteenth century) was one of prosperity, peace, and territorial expansion under three brilliant Manchu Emperors—K'ang Hsi, Yung Cheng, and Ch'ien Lung. It was a time of splendour and stability which excited the admiration of European missionaries, but there were no innovations. The Manchus were extremely conservative. Orthodoxy was the keynote, and new ideas and devices such as those brought by European traders and priests were given no respect.

In spite of their complete assimilation into Chinese culture the Manchu Emperors forbade their people to marry Chinese. They remained distinct as officials and soldiers, many of them unfitted for their posts especially when compared to Chinese scholars, who were qualified for but debarred from official appointments. But such weaknesses as these did not reveal themselves in the eighteenth century, a period when China under foreign rule achieved a pinnacle of splendour and power. Yet in the hundred years which followed, the brilliance of these days turned to weakness, misrule, and cultural atrophy. China's greatness in the eighteenth century became her delusion. When George III of England sent Lord Macartney as his ambassador to the Manchu Court at Peking in 1793 the old Emperor Ch'ien Lung treated him as a barbarian bearing tribute. The Confucian Empire admitted of no equals. It was this arrogance and blind refusal to accept change of any kind which was to bring about China's downfall.

The enormous expansion of industry and commerce which followed the Industrial Revolution brought Western influence, especially British, to every corner of the earth. Ever since it was established in the reign of Queen Elizabeth the East India Company claimed a monopoly of all trade to the Eastern seas. It was a monopoly granted by the Crown to prevent competition between British merchants, but the Dutch and French in their own chartered companies challenged the British. Having established themselves firmly in India, the British Company began to develop the China trade in the seventeen-eighties. The demand in Europe for Chinese tea and silk expanded greatly at this time. New and faster sailing vessels called 'tea clippers' sailed from England and from Massachusetts in America, all heading for one port in China, Canton. In smaller numbers merchant ships of Holland, Germany, Denmark, and Spain sailed to China, mostly for her tea and silk but also for her porcelain, ivories, and jade which became much in demand by wealthy people.

At the beginning of the nineteenth century the balance of this trade was very much in China's favour. As the demand for tea and silk increased it became more and more difficult for the European merchants to meet the cost by sales of European or

Map of East Asia in Dr. Sun's time with some recent changes in place names in brackets.

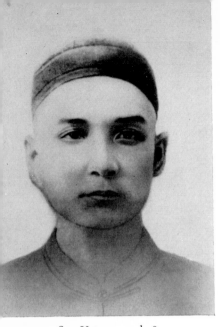

Sun Yat-sen aged 18.

His mother.

Choyhang village in Kwangtung Province, his birthplace.

A family or clan temple in Canton said to have been used as secret headquarters of the Hsing Chung Hui. The characters read: 'Wang Family Academy'.

Sun in his thirties.

Camera Press

The Chinese Legation in London.

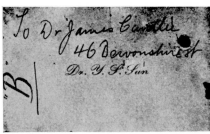

To Dr James Cantlie
46 Devonshire St
Dr. Y. L. Sun
Please take care of the messenger from me at present, he is very poor and will lost his work by doing for me.

To Dr James Cantlie
46 Devonshire St
Dr. Y. S. Sun

I was kidnapped into the Chinese Legation on sunday, & shall be smuggled out from England to China for death Pray rescue me quick?

a ship is already charter by the C.L. for the service to take me to China and I shall be locked up all the way without communication to any body. O! Woe to me!

Messages written by Sun, while in captivity in the Legation, to
Sir James Cantlie.

Indian goods. Cloth and other manufactures of the new industrial age in England appealed little to the Chinese. In consequence payment had to be made in silver. But by the opening of the century a new commodity for sale to the Chinese was found—opium. Opium was not a new drug to the Chinese. The opium poppy was cultivated in the mountains of Yunnan and Szechuan in west China. But its import through Canton now grew rapidly and the habit of smoking the drug increased alarmingly.

The opium trade was illegal in China. The East India Company did not officially recognize its existence, and in fact much of the opium was carried by 'country' vessels trading from India where the opium was grown and not by the Company's clippers. But there was no doubt that the Company shared in the profits. Great profits also accrued to Chinese merchants and officials who made no attempt to enforce the law against the traffic. Even in Peking itself profit from the opium trade was tacitly welcomed.

The widespread smoking of opium was not only injurious to health but its mass import had also caused a complete reversal in terms of trade. Now the export of tea and silk was not enough to pay for the opium, and Chinese silver flowed from the country in exchange. By 1832 the annual import of opium had risen to over twenty thousand chests.

The Manchu emperors had confined all foreign trade to Canton from the end of the seventeenth century. Their attitude was summed up by the Emperor Ch'ien Lung when he terminated Lord Macartney's unsuccessful embassy with these words:

'The Celestial Empire possesses all things in prolific abundance and lacks no product within its borders. There is therefore no need to import the manufactures of outside barbarians in exchange for our own products.'

The foreign merchants who came to Canton were isolated. They were confined to a narrow strip of land on the banks of the Pearl River, living in their warehouses or 'factories' without access to the city. They had no contact with the Governor of

Canton or any other officials. All transactions were conducted through a group of Chinese called the Hong Merchants selected by the Commissioner of Customs. Wealthy merchants and directors of the British East India Company had to address 'petitions' in humiliating terms for any request. There was no question of equality.

There were other vexations for the despised foreigners. They were not allowed to employ Chinese servants nor to learn the Chinese language. European women were not allowed to come to Canton. At the end of the summer season when the ships sailed home the merchants were required to leave Canton and stay in the Portuguese colony of Macao, down the river.

Bribery and corruption flourished. Chinese officials were paid handsomely for conniving at the illegal import of opium. Arbitrary levies on all cargoes were determined by what the corrupt commerce could stand. Sailors, after the boredom of a six months voyage, got involved in drunken brawls with Chinese and murders were commonplace.

The British Government viewed this state of profitable chaos with concern. In 1834 the monopoly of the East India Company was ended and trade became open to anybody. In the same year Lord Palmerston, the Foreign Secretary, appointed Lord Napier to be the Chief Superintendent of British Trade in China. Napier was required to reside in Canton, and to open discussions with the Governor of Kwangtung on all matters affecting the Canton trade. Arriving with his wife and children and a large suite, Lord Napier addressed himself by letter, not petition, directed to the Governor. He was ignored. Threats, mutual insults, and finally suspension of trade and a siege of the 'factories' led to the complete failure of the Napier mission. He died in Macao a few months after his arrival in China.

A few years later this impossible situation was resolved by war between Britain and China, the so-called Opium War of 1839–42. In 1839, in spite of enormous profits to the official purse, the Emperor decided to suppress the opium trade. He appointed a man of unusual ability, Lin Tse-hsu, to be his Special Commissioner in Canton. Lin set about his task with energy. He called upon Captain Charles Elliot, who had succeeded Lord Napier as British Superintendent, to require all opium held by his compatriots to be surrendered immediately. Elliot agreed but asked for compensation. Each merchant was called upon to sign an undertaking that he would cease to carry opium into Canton. The opium was given up but the guarantees were not signed. Elliot wanted to negotiate a new trading arrangement quite apart from opium. He wanted to improve conditions of living and trading at Canton or obtain an island off the coast where merchants and seamen could live and work without irksome Chinese controls. Lin was intransigent. He had seized the opium but he was unwilling to concede better trading arrangements or a position of equality to the British emissary.

Hostilities broke out later that year. In all the small engagements, mainly between British warships and Chinese war junks or shore batteries, China was defeated. The war was carried to the Yangtze River and finally in 1842 peace was concluded by the Treaty of Nanking. For China it was the beginning of a new era.

China had been forced open to trade. The Treaty of Nanking with the British was followed quickly by others with the Americans and several European powers. These treaties opened four more ports to foreign trade, Shanghai and Ningpo at the mouth of the Yangtze, and Foochow and Amoy in the province of Fukien. In each port, including Canton, small pieces of territory called 'concessions' were set aside for foreigners and 'extraterritoriality' was granted to them. This provided for their trial by their own consular representatives when they committed crimes. China's sovereignty was infringed. Customs duties on imports and exports were levied according to agreed scales. And the opium trade continued to flourish. The Treaty of Nanking ceded to Britain Hong Kong, a small island off the coast of Kwangtung which had been invested during the fighting.

These were the first of the 'unequal treaties' which were to be the subject of Chinese bitterness against the West for the next hundred years. Through the 'treaty ports' which were opened in the forties, and others later in the century on the Yangtze and in

the north, came economic change and development. Besides
trade came the slow and reluctant realization among the Chinese
that there were other civilizations as well as their own and that
the most powerful was that represented by the white-faced 'ocean
devils'. These economic changes had their greatest effect in the
south and central region. On the coast and in cities on the Yangtze
wealth and population expanded. New techniques of commerce
and industry were developed. It was in the south too that Western
ideas circulated and stimulated latent anti-Manchu sentiment. In
Imperial Peking life went on as usual even after the city had been
captured by a punitive expedition of British and French troops in
1860. The Manchu Court remained conservative, dignified, and
orthodox, still believing that the only way for China was that of
the Confucian Empire.

The last great emperor of China, Ch'ien Lung, had abdicated
in 1795 and died in 1799. From then onwards the Empire was
ruled, or misruled, by a dreary succession of weak and incompetent monarchs. Precisely at a time when China needed great
statesmen to confront the Western nations she found herself
without leadership. In the Forbidden City in Peking, the inner
palaces of the Imperial Court, the Emperor became more and
more the prisoner of his eunuchs. These custodians of the royal
harems manipulated affairs of state by intrigue, corruption, and
assassination, and they had far more influence than the scholar
officials at the capital.

Corruption among officials and tax-collectors was widespread.
As the century advanced discontent with Manchu mandarins and
the 'Bannermen', the Manchu garrisons, began to spread,
especially in the south. Poverty among the peasants was widespread. The population had increased dramatically in the eighteenth century and the beginning of the nineteenth. Secret
societies, such as the White Lotus and the Triad, were set up to
overthrow the Manchus and restore the native Ming Dynasty,
and by mid-century a great rebellion had broken out.

Revolts by peasants or military men against the reigning dynasty
were not uncommon in Chinese history. It was almost a process
of nature that a ruling house should decline into effete corrup-

tion and thus lose the Mandate of Heaven. Mencius, the most famous, after the Master, of all the Confucian philosophers, had evolved a theory of rebellion in the fourth century before Christ. Orthodox doctrine exalted the Emperor, the Son of Heaven, into an infallible demi-god, but his mandate to rule was cancelled when he lost virtue. In the nineteenth century by the time of Sun Yat-sen's birth, it was clear that the Ch'ing house had lost all virtue, certainly all energy and wisdom. Mencius might have justified revolt.

The great rebellion of the century was one of southern peasants led by a scholar who had failed in the imperial examinations for the civil service. He was Hung Hsiu-ch'uan, a schoolmaster of Kwangtung province. He became the founder of a religious society which was Christian although not orthodox or associated with any of the missionary sects. During an illness in 1837 Hung had a vision in which he saw himself destined to lead his people in a religious crusade against the Manchu emperors. He had met no Christian missionaries—for they were not yet allowed in the interior of China—but he had read translations from the Bible and copies of Protestant tracts which seemed to confirm his vision of a divine summons.

Hung Hsiu-ch'uan moved to the neighbouring province of Kwangsi in the eighteen-forties. His Society of God Worshippers flourished among the poor peasants. Its purpose was economic reform as well as a religious crusade. Orders for its suppression were given by the Manchus, but Hung resisted and triumphed. He formed an army and proclaimed a new dynasty which he called the T'ai P'ing T'ien Kuo, the Great Peace Heavenly Kingdom, and by 1851 he had conquered most of Kwangsi and Kwangtung provinces and marched his peasant army north to the Yangtze River. The soft Bannermen garrisons fell quickly in central China and in 1853 Hung established himself as the T'ai P'ing emperor at Nanking. If he had marched north to Peking at this point it is almost certain that he would have overthrown the Manchu Dynasty, but instead he consolidated his realm on the Yangtze, preached his own kind of Protestant Christianity, and introduced agrarian and social reforms.

For a dozen years Hung maintained his power in Nanking. He had established a new dynasty based on three vital policies, economic reform, a religious crusade, and anti-Manchu nationalism. Land was to be owned communally and redistributed. Equitable taxes were levied. Women were to be given equal rights with men. Hung claimed to be 'the younger brother of Jesus', a claim which shocked orthodox missionaries. His attitude to the Trinity was scarcely normal but his principles were Christian and he made many converts. His anti-Manchu policy could not fail to be popular especially in the south. He sought to treat foreigners as equals and would have welcomed missionaries as fellow-Christians.

It was strange, therefore, that the T'ai P'ing rebellion was finally defeated in 1864 by Manchu armies led by a European, General Charles Gordon (later of Khartoum). France and Britain had concluded the Treaty of Tientsin in 1860 after defeating China. By this, further 'treaty ports' were opened and diplomatic missions could be established at Peking. By the same treaty Kowloon, a small piece of the mainland opposite Hong Kong, was leased to Britain. Perhaps it was because the Manchus were weak and pliable that the Western powers gave them support in the suppression of the T'ai P'ings. Had the rebellion succeeded, China's revival might have been accelerated by nearly a century. For although the revolt was different from all others because of its Christian basis, the T'ai P'ing movement did have the traditional elements of success. Hung and his followers had energy, reforming zeal, hatred of the effete Manchus, willingness to accept new ideas, and considerable organizing ability. Had they succeeded, the course of China's history in the second half of the nineteenth century would certainly have been very different and probably less tragic.

There were other revolts in mid-century. The most notable were those of the Muslims in China's far western provinces, Sinkiang and Kansu. Although too far from Peking to overthrow the Manchu rulers these risings further weakened the Empire. Most of the great conquests of the Emperor Ch'ien Lung in the eighteenth century were slipping into anarchy or independence. At the same time the European powers were encroaching on the flanks of the Empire. France took over authority in Annam on the southern frontier in 1895. Russia, pushing her empire eastwards across the vast plains of Siberia, was challenging China's weak authority in Manchuria, the original home of the Manchus. By the eighteen-nineties Russian influence dominated the whole of the region to the north-east of Peking. Her trans-Siberian railway reached the Pacific and a branch line crossed Manchuria. While the maritime powers of Europe enforced their will on China through the 'unequal treaties' on the seaboard and in the Yangtze basin a new and even greater threat developed, imperialist Japan.

Japan, like China, had resisted Western influence. She had closed herself against European trade for more than two hundred years. Christians were persecuted. A feudal system prevailed, giving power to great landlords and a military class under a hereditary ruler. The Emperor was no more than a symbol. Quite suddenly, Japan was forced open. With a show of naval strength in 1854 the Americans compelled the Japanese to give their ships refuge in storm and facilities to trade. A decade later (1868) the authority of the Emperor was restored, the feudal power of landlords and soldiers destroyed, and Japan went straight ahead with a programme of Westernization. She began to industrialize and to reform her education and government, and quickly created a modern army and navy.

In 1894 Japan went to war with China over who should have authority in Korea. Korea was a Chinese protectorate but the Manchu armies were completely beaten, and by the Treaty of Shimonoseki in 1895 Korea was declared independent although in fact Japan had secured control of the country. By the same treaty she gained the Chinese island of Formosa (Taiwan). Japan had begun a half-century of war and domination over China which only ended in her own defeat in 1945.

So the last decade of the nineteenth century saw China in the extremities of defeat and humiliation. Partition by the Western powers and Japan seemed imminent. Germany obtained concessions in the north-eastern province of Shantung, France

in Kwangtung, and, as we have seen, Britain was given a
ninety-nine years lease of territory adjoining her colony of Hong
Kong. Russia and Japan competed for power over Manchuria.
China's foreign trade was completely in foreign hands. Foreign
gun-boats patrolled her rivers.

The Court at Peking was helpless. A succession of weak
emperors did nothing to save the country. On the contrary, they
resisted change and reform and preserved a mere fiction of
authority. They persisted in the belief that only Confucianism
was the correct way for China and that all new ideas and techniques brought by the Western powers were barbarian novelties.
The Emperor Ch'ien Lung had left a great empire. His successors Chia Ching and Tao Kwong who reigned in the first half
of the nineteenth century are known only for the troubles and
disasters which their ineptitude engendered—the rebellions of
secret societies, defeat by Britain in the Opium War, the indigni-
ties of the 'unequal treaties', and mounting impoverishment and
corruption. The Emperor Hsien Feng reigned from 1850 to 1861,
a period dominated by the T'ai P'ing rebellion and Western wars.
For a time his capital was invested by British and French troops.
The next two emperors were minors and power was given to a
regent, the favourite concubine of the late Emperor Hsien Feng.
Her name was Tzu Hsi ('Motherly and Auspicious'), and she was
the last great personality of imperial China.

Tzu Hsi was beautiful, cunning, and ruthless. She had a taste
for poetry and painting but no qualms in assassinating her op-
ponents. She hated foreigners and despised them. Chinese
Christians and reformers were equally intolerable. She ruled in
the minority of T'ung Chih and when he died prematurely the
successor to the throne was another child, the Emperor Kwang
Hsu. He too became the creature of the Empress Dowager. But
at the age of twenty he saw the truth of China's calamity: China
must reform or be destroyed. Most scholar officials were as conservative as their Manchu masters for reform meant the end of
their power and prestige, but there was one scholar of outstand-
ing ability who demanded a change. He was K'ang Yu-wei, a
Cantonese like Sun Yat-sen but, unlike Sun, a reformer, not a

revolutionary. He wanted to preserve the Manchu monarchy. The young Emperor Kwang Hsu accepted his advice and in 1898 issued with K'ang's help a whole series of edicts to reform the administration, the law, and education. Industry was to be promoted and a modern army created. These were the Hundred Days of Reform, but this last hope for China was extinguished by the Empress Dowager. She arrested the Emperor, cancelled the edicts, killed a number of reformers, and would have dealt with K'ang Yu-wei in the same manner had he not been able to escape to Japan. With the Emperor a prisoner in a palace of the Forbidden City and China in grave distress the Empress Dowager, ageing but serene, resumed her control of the Court, oblivious to everything. Two years later she had a great revolt on her hands, the Boxer Rebellion, but with wonderful skill she deflected the attack from the Manchu throne to the foreigners, especially their Christian missionaries and diplomats.

The Boxer Rebellion was the last event in a century of shame and defeat. It was a peasant rising in the north against misrule and poverty. They called themselves the Regiment of Righteous Harmony, practised gymnastics (hence the name Boxers), and held superstitious notions such as their invulnerability to bullets. The Empress Tzu Hsi persuaded them that their troubles were due to foreigners and they began to massacre Christians, missionaries, and Chinese converts. The killing was encouraged by the Empress. The Boxers had operated in the provinces around the capital and finally, with full support from the Throne, they attacked the foreign Legations in Peking. For three months in the summer of 1900 the legations were under siege—then an international force relieved the diplomats from likely massacre. Tzu Hsi with her captive Emperor fled to the west of China. It was her last, futile gesture of blind Manchu arrogance.

3

SUCCESS AND FAILURE

IN 1892, seven years before the outbreak of the Boxer Rebellion, Sun Yat-sen graduated from the Hong Kong Medical School. His class was the first to qualify and Sun was its most distinguished student. It was an event of importance for China as well as Sun for it marked her entry into modern medicine. Chinese had already qualified as doctors in Western universities but the Medical School at Hong Kong brought modern science to China herself.

Young and confident, Dr. Sun went to practise in Macao. There he was very near his family in Choyhang village. His father had died a few years earlier but his mother was still living in the village with other members of the family. In the year before Sun graduated, he had become the father of his only son whom he called Sun Fo. In Macao Sun Yat-sen was given facilities to practise in a clinic run by traditional-style Chinese doctors. This seems incredible as there was scepticism and even hostility among indigenous doctors to Western medicine but we know it from Sun's own account of the matter. He was a successful doctor. He performed major operations, sometimes with the help of his tutor Dr. Cantlie who came over from Hong Kong to assist him. But the Portuguese did not recognize his qualifications and in less than a year Sun moved to Canton. There too his practice of medicine was short-lived.

In Canton he was closer to the chaos and corruption of Manchu administration. He joined the Young China Party, at first a modest reform movement which soon became a focus for revolution with Sun one of its leaders. Less than two years after qualifying as a doctor Sun Yat-sen decided to give up his profession and devote his life to politics.

With a friend from his own village of Choyhang, Lu Ho-tung, he went to north China to see things for himself. It was 1894, the year of the outbreak of the Sino-Japanese War. With extraordinary naïveté and arrogance the two young men presented a memorandum on reform to the Viceroy of the northern provinces, Li Hung-chang, who had acquired a reputation for enlightened views as well as being the Emperor Kwang Hsu's senior adviser. The document called for reform in education, agriculture, and law. Not surprisingly it was ignored and Sun was refused an audience. Calls for reform from more mature and responsible heads had already disturbed the equanimity of the Imperial Court, especially the writings of K'ang Yu-wei. Sun and Lu returned south convinced that only revolution could remedy the situation.

Sun sailed to Hawaii. Revolutions need money as well as men and it was from the overseas Chinese that Sun was able to finance his risings in China and his political parties in and out of China in the next two decades. From the comfortable home of his brother Ah Mei, near Honolulu, Sun organized a branch of the Hsing Chung Hui, the Prosper China Society, with himself as chairman. In a few months he had more than a hundred members, nearly all of them Cantonese like the Sun brothers. The overt aims of the society were reform, but the secret and principal purpose was the overthrow of the dynasty.

The secret oath of the membership included the declaration 'Drive out the Manchus, restore the nation and establish a republic.' The older and much larger Triad Society had sought to overthrow the Ch'ing and restore the Ming dynasty. Sun's movement was to abolish dynastic rule and create the Chinese Republic. For the next ten years branches of the Hsing Chung Hui all over the world were to be the nuclei of the revolution.

In January 1895 Sun Yat-sen went to Hong Kong and immediately established a branch of the society. By March the Hong Kong branch had decided to attempt an armed rising in Canton. Sun and a man named Yang Chu-yun were the leading organizers. Together with members of the Young China Party in Canton it was planned to start the revolt on 26 October at the time of the grave-tending festival. This, the 'first revolutionary attempt' seems to have been a model of bad planning. China had just been defeated by Japan in the north, the Manchu garrison in Canton was weak, the police corrupt, and discontent was widespread—ideal conditions for rebellion. It is true that the rebels had difficulty in obtaining arms. Six hundred pistols were to be shipped from Hong Kong. On the same river boat were to come four hundred men to join the force in Canton. Two further groups, one from Swatow in the north-east of Kwangtung province and another from the West River were to march on the capital simultaneously. The Society in Hong Kong chose the first 'President of the Provisional Government'—Yang, not Sun. Yang, the senior by seven years, was thirty-five.

A few days before the 26th Sun went to Canton. All was ready. Then news came that the Swatow group were held up. Orders were given to postpone the rising till the 28th. Sun sent a telegram to Yang to delay the sailing of the Hong Kong contingent. Then the Manchu authorities heard about the plot and three suspects were arrested. Panic developed among the rebels. Sun's telegram to Hong Kong arrived too late and Yang dispatched his men up the Pearl River. On arrival at Canton they were seized along with the pistols and ammunition. The first revolutionary attempt had failed. Forty-five men were executed, including Lu Ho-tung who had accompanied Sun to the north the previous year. Sun himself had the narrowest escape. With a price on his head he first went down-river to Macao and then to Hong Kong. He saw his friend Cantlie and sailed for Japan for it was too dangerous to stay in Hong Kong. He had begun his revolutionary career in earnest.

In Japan Sun cut off his queue. The custom among Chinese men of wearing their hair long in a pig-tail and shaving the front part of the head had been introduced by the Manchus in the seventeenth century. To cut it off as Sun now did was an act of political defiance. At the same time it served his safety, for having also discarded the gown and little black hat in favour of Western dress, Sun became, according to his own account, indistinguishable from the Japanese. Having made contact with some Chinese students and shopkeepers in Yokohama Sun sailed once again to Honolulu. Here he was safe and could have settled as a doctor but there was no question of settling down. In Hawaii he could get money for the revolution. In the United States and Europe there were Chinese students to be mobilized for the fight. In June 1896 Sun sailed for America.

In San Francisco he organized a branch of the Hsing Chung Hui, but it was hard going as most of his compatriots were more interested in business than politics. He spoke to any Chinese he could find in his progress across the continent. All the way he was followed by agents of the Manchus. At the end of September he sailed from New York on board the British vessel *Majestic* and arrived at Liverpool on 30 September. He went straight to London.

London and Europe were necessary for Sun's revolutionary education. He was thirty, a doctor of medicine, and a rebel with one unsuccessful rebellion to his credit. But he was politically immature. Europe was not only the centre of the world, it was also the mother of revolutions. Sun had the will to learn and enough money from his brother and the movement to support himself in comfort for a long stay. There were Chinese students to be converted, but most of his time was to be spent in the reading room of the British Museum.

On arrival in London he put up at Haxell's Hotel in the Strand. He went to his friends, Dr. and Mrs. Cantlie, who had returned to England and lived at 46 Devonshire Street. He was warmly welcomed and spent a good deal of the first week in London with them and Dr. Manson. The Cantlies helped him to find lodgings at 8 Gray's Inn Place in Holborn, took him to church, and showed him the sights. For the first ten days Sun Yat-sen enjoyed the museums and galleries, the famous buildings, the extraordinary traffic in the streets, and the bourgeois comfort of his West End friends. But on Sunday, 11 October, things took a different turn.

He was walking to the Cantlies to accompany them to church when a Chinese approached and asked him if he was Chinese and from which province. Sun found himself talking to a fellow-Cantonese. The man was affable and invited him to his lodgings. Sun declined; he was on his way to church. Then a second Chinese came. He too invited Sun to his lodgings for a friendly chat. They were in Portland Place. Suddenly they stopped outside number 49, the door opened and they pushed Sun inside. He was a captive in the Chinese Legation.

In Sun's account *Kidnapped in London* he shows surprising naïveté over this part of the incident. A fugitive with a price on his head might be expected to look out for trouble. Sun had no suspicion of these Chinese in the street and even inside the building it took him some time to realize that he was a prisoner of the Manchus.

He was taken to a room on the second floor at the back of the building. Several Chinese officials came into the room, then an Englishman. This was Sir Halliday Macartney, the Counsellor of the Legation. It was not uncommon at that time for the legations of Asian countries to employ Europeans in senior diplomatic positions. Sun describes the occasion:

'An old gentleman with white hair and a beard came into the room in rather a bumptious fashion and said, "Here is China for you; you are now in China." Sitting down, he proceeded to interrogate me, asking what my name was. I replied, "Sun." "Your name," he replied, "is Sun Wen. We had a telegram from the Chinese Minister in America informing us that you are a passenger to this country by the S.S. *Majestic* and the Minister asks me to arrest you."'

Macartney then asked Sun to write a note to his lodgings to have his clothes and papers brought to the Legation. Sun saw the danger this would bring to his friends in China, for he had names of rebels among his papers. He refused and asked that the note should go to Cantlie or Manson but Macartney could not accept and nothing was done. They left him alone in the room, fixed another lock on the door, and posted two guards outside. An English servant brought him food. There were more visits by interrogators and by Macartney, who told him that he was to be shipped back to China and executed. He would go on a ship of the Glen Line which was sailing soon and would be taken to the docks at night in secrecy on the pretext that he was a lunatic.

Sun spent the next few days trying to get notes to Cantlie. He gave them to the Chinese or English servants, but they were all handed to Macartney or to the Minister of the Legation, a man named Kung whom Sun never met. Then he tried throwing notes out of the window towards the house next door. This was discovered and the window barred. At the end of a week things looked hopeless. Then his Christian faith came to the rescue:

'My despair was complete and only by prayers to God could I gain any comfort. Still the dreary days and still more dreary nights wore on, and but for the comfort afforded me by prayer I believe I should have gone mad. After my release I related to Dr. Cantlie how prayer was my one hope, and told him how I should never forget the feeling that seemed to take possession of me as I rose from my knees on the morning of Friday, October 16th—a feeling of calmness, hopefulness, and confidence that assured me my prayer was heard and filled me with hope that all would be well.'

That day he had success. He persuaded an English servant named Cole to take a message to Cantlie. He pleaded with him to rescue a fellow-Christian from an unjust death and to reinforce the plea gave him all the money he had, no less than £20. Late that night Cantlie found this message slipped under his front door:

'There is a friend of yours imprisoned in the Chinese Legation here since last Sunday; they intend sending him out to China where it is certain they will hang him. It is very sad for the poor man, and unless something is done at once he will be taken away and no one will know it. I dare not sign my name, but this is the truth, so believe what I say. Whatever you do must be done at once or it will be too late. His name is, I believe, Sin Yin Sen.'

Cantlie went immediately to the police, first to Marylebone and then Scotland Yard. They were incredulous and in any case they could not interfere with the diplomatic immunity of a foreign legation. Cantlie went to the Foreign Office who were equally unhelpful. The next day when he was with Dr. Manson discussing their plans, a message was delivered to him. This time it was from Sun himself:

'I was kidnapped on Sunday last by two Chinamen and forcibly taken into the Chinese Legation. I am imprisoned and in a day or two I am to be shipped off to China on board a specially chartered vessel. I am certain to be beheaded. O! Woe is me!'

Time seemed to be running out. Cantlie and Manson hired a private detective to keep watch on the Legation. They decided to enlist the help of the Press and went to the *Times*. But the *Times* declined to publish the story. The *Globe* was of different metal and came out with the headline 'Chinese Revolutionary Kidnapped in London'. Here was a story for the late Victorian imagination with its romantic notions of unknown China. Rumours circulated about torture and poisoned food. A rebel against tyranny was to be deported to his death. Crowds gathered in Portland Place, and Lord Salisbury, the Foreign Secretary, advised the Legation to give up Sun. Macartney held firmly to the principle of diplomatic immunity and claimed that Sun had gone to the Legation by choice.

But China was in no position to worsen relations with Britain over such a trifling matter. The public scandal which the case quickly became, together with the British Government's request, persuaded the Legation to yield. Twelve days after his seizure Sun Yat-sen came out of the Chinese Legation to the cheers of London well-wishers. The Cantlies, the Press, and public made a great fuss of him. For a few days he was a little hero whose escape from oriental tyranny and death had been contrived by the pressure of public opinion. Sun himself was delighted with his fame. In *Kidnapped in London* he records every detail of his triumph—the clamouring Press reporters, the letters in the *Times*, the goodwill of the London public, and the affectionate care of the Cantlies.

For the next two years Sun lived obscurely in London with occasional long excursions to the Continent. His brother Ah Mei faithfully supplied him with a modest income and money seems to have come too from branches of the Hsing Chung Hui in Hawaii and Hong Kong. He spent most of his time in the reading room of the British Museum, reading politics, economics,

Sun leaving Shanghai for Nanking to become Provisional President of the
Republic.

Sun pays his respects at the Ming Tombs near Nanking, February 1912.

Tzu Hsi, the Empress Dowager.

Yuan Shih-k'ai.

From Toyo Bunkashi Daikei, Volume VII (*Seibundo, Tokyo*). By courtesy of Henry Mc⸝

Mao Tse-tung (right) and Chou En-lai.

Camera Press

From F. Krarup Nielsen The
Dragon Awakes (*The Bodley
Head*)

Mikhail Borodin.

Chiang Kai-shek and Sun at the opening
of the Whampoa Military Academy, Canton.

a

b

c

d

a   The first Mrs. Sun.

b   Sun in his mid-fifties at his desk in Shanghai.

c   The second Mrs. Sun after her husband's deat
F. Krarup Nielsen The Dragon Awakes (*The Bodley Head*)

d   Sun with his second wife on the way to Pekin
in the winter of 1924–25, his last journey.

agriculture, military science, and many other subjects. He found special interest in Henry George and Karl Marx. All revolutions fascinated him but it is doubtful that he understood all of what he read. His comments in later speeches and writings show an ingenuous and superficial grasp of Europe's social problems. He may have met Lenin in these years; he certainly met other Russian exiles with whom he discussed the coming revolutions, Chinese and Russian. He met Chinese students in Brussels, Paris, and Berlin, but he had little success in persuading them to join the cause. It is not surprising. Although a revolutionary, Sun had no policy except the overthrow of the Manchu Dynasty. He wanted a republic, but he had not yet worked out its constitution. He was a rebel but a believing Christian. But he had extraordinary will-power, his greatest asset.

After two years apprenticeship to the theory of revolution, Sun returned to the East. He had heard of the Hundred Days Reform and the *coup d'état* which foiled the plans of Emperor Kwang Hsu and the scholar-politician Kang Yu-wei. But instead of going to the support of the reformer, Sun returned—this time to Japan—in open enmity to Kang, proclaiming one objective, the violent end of the monarchy.

Yokohama was his headquarters. His troops, if he could win them, were the hundreds of Chinese students at Japanese universities. His fellow-generals were the more radical reformers who had escaped the executioner's sword, leaders of secret societies including his own, the Hsing Chung Hui, and some Japanese liberals. He was not the undisputed leader but the episode in London had increased his fame and his uncompromising stand appealed to students.

The defeat of the Boxers in the summer of 1900 had humiliated China and still further weakened the Manchu throne. Sun decided to strike again in his native south. He bought ammunition from the Philippines where an independence movement had just failed. He got money from compatriots in Hong Kong and Hanoi, as well as Japan, and sent his friend Cheng Shih-liang to Waichow in eastern Kwangtung to arm and mobilize a force of peasants and march on Canton. Help was even offered from

Japanese-occupied Formosa but it never came. This, the 'second revolutionary attempt' failed like the first one through inadequate planning and lack of ammunition. Cheng raised a considerable force in Waichow and marched on Canton. But the support of the rebels in the provincial capital was ill-timed and half-hearted. Considering the weakness of the Manchu garrison, especially in morale, it is surprising that the revolt had so little success. After some initial progress, Cheng disbanded his troops long before they reached Canton and made for Hong Kong. He was captured and executed.

With extraordinary bravado Sun commented on the defeat:

'We are not in the least depressed over the result. Quite the reverse, in fact, as it shows us how easily the imperial troops can be defeated as soon as our men are properly armed and prepared for the great effort.'

Conceit as well as indomitable will-power was one of Sun's most notable characteristics.

Soon after this little revolt in the far-away south the Court at Peking embarked on an extraordinary series of reforms. The Boxer defeat, the propaganda of the reformers, especially Kang Yu-wei and Liang Shih-chao, and the obvious facts of political life, compelled Tzu Hsi, the stubborn old Empress, to do something at last. From 1901 until her death in 1908 the very measures which she had suppressed by execution and tyranny in 1898 were now promulgated. Universities and schools of the Western type were opened. The modernization of the army and navy were started. In 1905 the old examinations for the civil service, based on Confucian scholarship, were abolished. And, even more drastic, plans were made to establish a National Assembly and Provincial Assemblies which would eventually have elected members. It might have been expected that these reforms would satisfy the demands of the reformers and weaken the cause of revolution. But corruption among officials, incompetence, and the break-down of effective government which China was now suffering prevented the success of these long-overdue reforms. If the Court now seemed willing to reform it completely lacked the power to carry through the measures it advocated. Tzu Hsi pardoned some of the reformers whom she had arrested in 1898, but she would not allow the two leaders Kang Yu-wei and Liang Chih-chao to return to China. These men might have saved the monarchy which Sun so ardently wished to destroy.

Sun Yat-sen spent a good deal of his energy in opposing the reformers. In a letter to his compatriots in Hawaii he wrote:

'You are accustomed to believing that the revolution and the pro-gramme of the reform party are exactly the same, though different in name. You indulge in the belief that the reform party is carrying the cause of the revolution under the name of protecting the imprisoned Emperor. But I assure you that you are wrong.'

In another letter he says:

'I have been engaged in a hard struggle against the reform party.... I intend to travel wherever there are Chinese and I believe that in three or four months I shall succeed in overcoming them all.'

And so, at the end of 1903 he left Japan and set off on his second world tour. Sun's restless propensity for travel might not appear to help the cause of violent rebellion but it could promote two vital objectives—the raising of money and winning the allegiance of the new intellectuals, the Chinese students in America and Europe.

He addressed meetings of Chinese in Honolulu. He obtained entry to the United States by declaring that he had been born in Hawaii (revolutionary ends justify means) and embarked on a speaking campaign among Chinese right across the States. There was more interest in reform than revolution, but Sun had some success in raising money and in forming branches of his Hsing Chung Hui, the Prosper China Society. He went on to Europe. He wrote later:

'When I visited Europe for the second time in 1905 the majority of Chinese students had come to believe in revolution. Thereupon I sounded the clarion call by announcing the Three Principles of the People and the Five-Power Constitution which I had long cherished.'

Things had moved since his British Museum days. Chinese students were awakened and eager to join the fight. And Sun himself had developed a political philosophy. But it was not until 1924, a year before his death, that he set forth his political thinking in coherent form. His political creed was then to become China's national doctrine for the next quarter of a century.

Sun returned to a Japan which had just defeated Imperial Russia. Manchuria, part of China's territory, was the battle-field and the *casus belli*. Japan, having defeated weak China ten years earlier, now took on a 'white' nation whose expansion across Siberia conflicted with her own. Russia's greatest defeat was at sea but it was Manchu China which suffered most, losing to Japan authority over her own north-eastern territory and what remained of her dignity. The Chinese students in Japan gave Sun a great welcome. Revolution and Westernization could do for China what Japan had achieved.

Sun now assumed leadership of the revolutionary movement among the Chinese in Japan. There had been another armed revolt when he had been in Europe, this time in the province of Hunan in south-central China. Although it failed, the Hunan attempt had been better led than those in Kwangtung. The leader had been Hwang Hsing who was later to be Sun's military man and who now joined him as a fugitive in Japan. There were others—Wang Ching-wei, who became China's puppet Prime Minister under the Japanese in 1940, Hu Han-min, later to be a leading figure in the Nationalist Government, and Sung Chiao-jen a colleague of Hwang in the Hunan rising. Sun seized the opportunity created by rising political feeling among overseas Chinese to launch a new political party. This was the Tung Meng Hui, the Alliance (Its full name was Chung-kuo Ke-ming Tung Meng Hui—the Chinese Revolutionary Alliance.)

The Tung Meng Hui was a fusion of a number of small societies with anti-Manchu objectives and the old Hsing Chung Hui. As well as proclaiming revolution and the end of the

Manchus, the party called for friendship with Japan, peace and co-operation with other nations, the creation of the Chinese republic, and—most significantly—the nationalization of the land. Here was the first sign of socialism, very likely the result of Sun's studies in the British Museum eight years earlier. The Tung Meng Hui was a much more serious political party than the older society. Branches were set up secretly all over China as well as among the overseas Chinese in Japan, Hong Kong, and in Singapore. It published an influential journal called the *Min Pao* (*People's Press*) which had a formidable influence among students. It lasted three years. Then in 1908, at the request of Peking the Japanese closed it down, as it was becoming embarrassing.

Meanwhile Sun was busy with violent revolution. Between 1906 and 1909 there were no less than six 'revolutionary attempts' organized by Sun and his Tung Meng Hui. All were in the southern provinces of Kwangtung, Kwangsi, and Yunnan, and all failed. It is surprising that these attempts had such poor success as the dynasty was tottering to an ignominious close. The T'ai P'ing leader Hung had infinitely more success half a century earlier when the Manchu power was still of some account. Sun was not proving to be a military leader but, in fairness, he was not supported by disciplined and efficient followers.

Near the close of 1908 the Empress Dowager died. A few hours before the end of the last great Manchu the young Emperor Kwang Hsu had also died. There were rumours that Tzu Hsi, who had held him captive since the coup of 1898, arranged his assassination; she could not bear the thought that he might win success at last. The rumour is at least in keeping with her ruthless career. The last of the Manchu Emperors ascended the throne, scarcely a year old. His reign title was Hsun Tung, his personal name Henry Pu Yi.

Sun's revolts were proving embarrassing to the places where he organized them. He had become unwelcome in Japan, banned from Hong Kong and from Hanoi. He now sailed again for Hawaii. This was the start of his third and last world tour. He spent a long time in Hawaii before going on to the States. An-

other revolt occurred in Kwangtung in 1910 and yet another in
the spring of 1911. This one was led by Hwang Hsing and became more famous than the rest. The rebels almost succeeded in
capturing Canton. Years later, on Yellow Flower Hill in the
suburbs of Canton, they built a monument to the dead heroes
of this attempt, the Seventy-two Martyrs. It was the last failure.

When the day of success came Sun Yat-sen was far from
China. It occurred on 10 October 1911, the Double Tenth which
was later to be celebrated as the National Day each year until
the establishment of the People's Republic in 1949. A bomb
exploded accidentally in Wuchang on the Yangtze. The secret
organization of the Tung Meng Hui in central China had made
great progress, especially in the provinces of Hupeh and Hunan.
Some of the Manchu garrisons were disaffected and joined in
the revolt. Wuchang was captured by the revolutionaries, the
cities of Hankow and Hanyang were bombarded. But the revolt
lacked both military and political leadership. Sun Yat-sen, the
obvious leader, was touring America and Hwang Hsing was in
Hong Kong. The young rebels in Wuchang—students and
soldiers—persuaded an Imperial officer, Li Yuan-hung, to lead
them. The rebellion continued along the Yangtze River and in
the southern provinces. They captured Nanking and the Chinese
sector of Shanghai (the major part being under international
control). Their forces rapidly increased by Imperial defections
and enthusiastic students. One young officer who joined them
was Chiang Kai-shek, later to be President of the Republic.

The situation was very different in Peking and the north.
There was no sympathy with the Tung Meng Hui and revolutionary ideas. But the Court was in panic. The Throne could be
saved by only one man, a man whom the old Empress Dowager
had used to suppress the reformers in 1898. This was Yuan
Shih-kai, a former viceroy of the northern provinces and the com-
mander of the only modern army in China. The Regent called
upon Yuan to suppress the revolt. Yuan agreed but delayed
moving his army south. He complained of indisposition, but in
fact he had realized that the monarchy must fall. In November
units of his army attacked the revolutionaries and gained some

success. Hankow was recaptured for the Imperial cause. China was now divided between north and south with a civil war raging along the banks of the Yangtze.

Sun Yat-sen had no part in the rebellion. Indeed, he seems to have been quite ignorant of its imminence according to his *Autobiography*:

'While the Wuchang Revolution was taking place I arrived at Denver, Colorado. About a fortnight before I had received a telegram from Hwang Hsing in Hong Kong. Because my secret code book was in my trunk, which had already gone to Denver, I had no way of translating it on the way. That night on arriving in Denver, I took out the secret code and decoded the telegram which read: "Chu Cheng arrived at Hong Kong from Wuchang reporting sympathizers in the New Army determined to move. Please remit funds at once." I was then in Denver and could think of no way to raise funds. I was thinking of wiring an answer: "Do not move" but it was late at night and I was extremely tired from the day's tedious travelling and I was confused in my thoughts. I thought I would have a good night's rest first and then would answer him next day after giving the matter some more thought. However, I slept until eleven o'clock the next morning. When I got up I was hungry. I went to a cafeteria to eat my breakfast. On passing a news-stand in the lobby I bought a newspaper which opened with the news: "Wuchang occupied by revolutionaries". All the difficulties involved in answering Hwang's telegram were completely removed. Consequently I sent a telegram to him explaining how my reply was delayed and telling him my plan. I immediately left for the eastern part of the United States.'

Seldom, if ever, could a revolutionary leader have written such a confession of unpreparedness. To be without his code book at such a time shows how ill-informed Sun was on the imminence of revolt. To go to bed after decoding it in the knowledge that the telegram had been written two weeks earlier may not have been so culpable since there was nothing he could do about the situation. The passage reveals Sun's *sang froid* and supreme self-confidence. He had no shame for his careless treatment of telegrams from the military leader at the front.

Instead of returning immediately to China to lead the rebellion,

Sun went to London and Paris. He had no status; the Manchu Government was recognized by the British and French. However, he claims to have influenced both countries in his favour and to have persuaded them to grant no loans to Peking. On his way east he was hailed as a hero at Singapore and when he reached Hong Kong it was already clear that he would assume leadership of the new Republic.

By the beginning of December an armistice had been arranged and by the middle of the month the two parties were in conference at Shanghai. Yuan sent delegates to represent him; he refused to expose himself to the dangers of the revolutionary south. He also knew that the revolutionaries could not defeat his army in the north. Sun Yat-sen arrived in Shanghai on 24 December 1911 acclaimed as the leader. On the 29th he went to Nanking in triumph; he had been elected by his fellow-revolutionaries to be the Provisional President of the Republic of China. The new nation was proclaimed on 1 January 1912.

The civil war was ended by the simple expedient of offering the Presidency to Yuan Shih-kai. Sun was in office only six weeks. In that period he had performed many ceremonies, made many speeches and demanded that the three-year-old Emperor should abdicate his throne. On 12 February the edict of abdication was published:

'From the preference of the people's heart the will of Heaven is discernible. How could we oppose the desires of millions for the glory of one family? Therefore we the Dowager Empress and the Emperor hereby vest the sovereignty in the people. Let Yuan Shih-kai inaugurate with full powers a provisional Republic and confer with the Republicans as to the ways in which we can assure peace to the Empire, thus forming a great Republic which will include the territories of Manchus, Chinese, Mongols, Mohammedans, and Tibetans.'

The Confucian Empire which had ruled China for more than two thousand years had come to an inglorious end.

Before leaving office President Sun Yat-sen went in solemn procession to the Ming tombs on the outskirts of Nanking. There, on the slopes of Purple Mountain at the end of an avenue of fabulous stone animals, he addressed himself in epic language to the spirits of the dead kings. The defeat of the Mings had been avenged, the Manchu usurpers were overthrown, and the Chinese had resumed dominion over their own land. Progress and happiness lay ahead, the spirits of the Ming Emperors could rest in peace. The ceremony was entirely within the Confucian tradition. It could have been expected from a new Emperor claiming legitimacy from a previous house but not from a revolutionary whose thinking was soon to be in sympathy with Russian Communism. Sun's nationalism sometimes compelled him to look back and become a traditionalist at variance with his own principles.

On the day after the abdication, 13 February 1912, Sun Yat-sen gave way to Yuan, calling him to come to Nanking to establish his government there. Yuan refused to move south. He claimed that there might be disorders in Peking if he left. He invited members of the revolutionary National Assembly to visit him in the north. Yuan was now declared the Provisional President but still refused to leave the old capital. His one qualification for leadership was his strength. He had no republican, far less democratic, sentiments. He was an autocrat with ambition and ability. Sun Yat-sen had yielded place to Yuan in order to unite the nation and put an end to the civil war. He believed that his life's work had been accomplished. Moreover, he was deceived into believing that Yuan was not only a strong and able man but also a leader who shared the same republican and patriotic views as himself. After long discussions with Yuan in Peking where Sun was treated—and flattered—like a royal guest, Sun sent a telegram to Hwang Hsing urging him to come to Peking and expressing support for his successor:

'Have talked with Yuan twice since my arrival in Peking. Regarding industries and related matters his ideas are the same as mine. As to defence and foreign policy our views are quite similar. According to my observations he is in a situation beyond suspicion and deserves our sympathy.'

Within a few months of this statement Sun was a political
exile in Japan. His extraordinary naïveté had been his undoing
again.

Sun had re-formed the Tung Meng Hui and created out of it
a new political party, the Kuomintang, the Nationalist Party,
in August 1912. Then, after his discussions with Yuan in Peking,
Sun virtually withdrew from politics. He was given, at his own
request, the inconspicuous post of Director of Railway Development. Sun had always laid stress on the importance of railways
in the economic growth of China. He toured the country and then
went to Shanghai to open his Railway Office.

With Sun Yat-sen safely out of the way in Shanghai drawing
the railway map of China, Yuan embarked on the destruction of
the Republic of which he was the Provisional President. He called
the National Assembly into session in Peking and persuaded
it to elect him as the permanent President of the Republic. By
the summer of 1913 he had arrested or assassinated those members
of the Kuomintang who seemed dangerous and then disbanded
the National Assembly. The most likely candidate for the post
of Prime Minister, Sung Chiao-jen, was murdered in Shanghai
as he was boarding a train for Peking. Yuan was almost certainly
behind the assassination. Sun Yat-sen gave up his railway planning and fled to Japan. Rebellion against Yuan broke out in Nanking and the south but it had no leadership and failed quickly.

The revolution had been betrayed. Yuan was in sole charge
in Peking and now set about the final act of perfidy—the establishment of a new Imperial Dynasty with himself as the Emperor. He
arranged for petitions calling him to ascend the throne. He performed the ceremony of ploughing at the Temple of Agriculture
and prepared to make sacrifices at the Altar of Heaven. All was
in readiness for the final ceremony when revolt broke out, far in
the south-west. His own army in Yunnan rose against him.
Students in Shanghai and Peking demonstrated. They denounced
intrigues with the Japanese who had demanded concessions, com-
mercial and military, throughout China. To older Chinese it
would have been quite natural and proper for a new dynasty to
arise out of the ruins of the Manchu house. A strong man had

come to assume the Mandate of Heaven. But at the last moment
Yuan Shih-kai held back in the face of revolt and popular hostility.
He died in the summer of 1916, leaving China in fragments of
disunity.

In 1914 Sun Yat-sen married for the second time. He was in
Japan, writing condemnations of Yuan and calling on his
comrades of the Kuomintang to unite for another effort. The
young lady, about half his age, was his secretary, Soong Ching-
ling, daughter of Charles Soong, a Methodist preacher with
American connections. There were three Soong daughters, all
beautiful and all talented. Of the three Ching-ling was the radical
who could believe in Sun's destiny and the Republic. Like Sun
she was aware of the deep social injustice of Chinese society.
Although educated in America like her sisters, Ching-ling became
a socialist. After Sun's death in 1925, she became a supporter
of the Communist Party and eventually a leading figure in the
Communist Government. The other sisters moved in a different
direction. Ai-ling married H. H. Kung who became Minister
of Finance in the Kuomintang Government and Mei-ling became the First Lady of Kuomintang China by marrying General
Chiang Kai-shek.

Although a professing Christian Sun married for a second time
without form of divorce. The other wife remained quietly in
obscurity in the south. By Chinese standards of those days she
had no cause for complaint. It was a normal happening, especially
when the husband led a life of political adventure. Although a
woman of intelligence and strong character the first Mrs. Sun
was essentially a peasant, quite unfitted for the kind of life her
husband lived. Ching-ling, on the other hand, was sophisticated
and cosmopolitan, spoke excellent English, and shared her
husband's revolutionary fervour.

Soon after Yuan's death, Sun Yat-sen returned to China, first
to Shanghai and later, in 1917, to Canton. Yuan had been succeeded by Li Yuan-hung, the army officer who had taken part
in the 1911 revolution in Wuchang, but Li's authority as President
scarcely reached the suburbs of Peking. China was in the period
of warlords, military adventurers whose armies owed them per-

sonal loyalty and who had no thoughts of democracy or patriot-
ism. With the death of Yuan, what was left of central authority
was removed. The generals whom he had named governors of
provinces became the tyrants of the areas dominated by their
personal armies. They fought among themselves, especially in
the northern provinces and in Manchuria. Their soldiers looted
towns and villages. China's economic plight was appalling.

An extraordinary incident occurred in Peking in 1917. One of
the warlords, a certain General Chang Hsun who had taken part
in the revolution, compelled President Li Yuan-hung to flee the
capital and actually reinstated the Emperor Pu Yi on the throne.
Kang-Yu-wei, the scholar reformer, supported the action, believing that monarchy was the right system for China. And so, for
nearly a week, the Ch'ing Dynasty was restored! The boy
Emperor, aged nine, was removed from his throne by the arrival
at the gates of Peking of another army led by a general with
less imperial inclinations than Chang.

Sun Yat-sen went to Canton. With some of the old guard of
the Kuomintang and young officers who had fought at
Wuchang he established a government. He called himself the
'Generalissimo' and for the first time assumed the role of a
military leader. For a while his army prospered. He staged a
series of campaigns in his native province of Kwangtung and
neighbouring Kwangsi. His aim was to secure the southern provinces and then march north. It was ten years later that the
Northern Expedition took place and triumphed, two years after
Sun had died.

Sun's first successes in Kwangtung were short-lived. One of his
own generals, Chen Chiung-ming, turned against him. Sun
narrowly escaped death. He was taken down the Pearl River in
a British gun-boat to Hong Kong. From there he returned to
his comfortable house in the French concession at Shanghai.
There, in 1918, Sun began to write his *Plans for National Reconstruction*.

By the end of the second decade of the twentieth century China
was in a desperate plight. The government in Peking had reluc-
tantly joined the Allies in the war against Germany but the peace

treaty at Versailles gave none of Germany's rights (mainly concessions in Shantung) to China. Instead her aggressive neighbour, Japan, took over Germany's privileges and made further demands, military and economic, in return for loans. Internationally China had gained nothing from her revolution. Foreigners still had extra-territorial rights exempting them from Chinese law. Small pieces of her territory on the coast and up the Yangtze River, the so-called 'concessions', were still ruled by foreign powers. Foreign gun-boats patrolled her rivers. Her dignity as a great nation was affronted. Within the country itself there was political chaos. The central government in Peking had little or no power over the provinces. That was in the irresponsible hands of warlords. Poverty increased with anarchy. But in the last few years of Sun Yat-sen's life new developments occurred which were to change the whole scene.

4

THE KUOMINTANG AND THE COMMUNISTS

Before we recount the events in the last few years of Sun Yat-sen's life, let us consider briefly the social and intellectual changes which were sweeping China just after the First World War. Behind the failure and violence of her politics, the corruption, power-lust, and ineptitude of her rulers, great changes were taking place. A new China was being born.

By the nineteen-twenties thousands of Chinese students had studied in the universities of Europe, America, and Japan. New schools and universities, the best of them run by missionaries, had been established all over China. Besides the techniques of science, medicine, and engineering these returned students and the new schools brought Western ideas into an old and decaying society. Japan had long since capitulated to the Western challenge. She had accepted the need for change and was now one of the great powers. It was clear to the young intellectuals that China must change too. But change to what? To a liberal democracy such as that of America or England with an elected Parliament? Or to a proletarian dictatorship like the one just established in the Soviet Union? If the young intellectuals were not sure which political path to follow they were at least certain that the old culture must be rejected.

The practice of Buddhism and Taoism had long since declined into mumbo-jumbo. Few men of education cared for these ancient systems of thought and religion. True, there were scholars who could understand the meaning of Tao and others who could lecture on Chinese Buddhism and its influence on art and poetry in the T'ang Dynasty. But those who still practised or believed in these faiths were the ignorant peasants or illiterate workers. Their simple, superstitious thinking degraded these religions. Buddhist and Taoist temples had become places for fortune-tellers, looked after by caretakers who charged a fee for their services, not by learned mystics.

The summit of the Confucian system which had sustained China for more than two thousand years was the Emperor. When he abdicated in 1912 this was the official sign that the tradition had reached its end. The practice of worshipping the spirits of ancestors continued, the family remained the central unit of society but only among the peasants and simple folk of the towns and cities. The new middle class might give lip-service to the Four Books but they were already following the bourgeois ways of the new capitalism which the Western world had brought to China. Without religion, without tradition, young China found herself in the dilemma of indecision, inspired only by one emotion —nationalism.

The changes which modern industry and commerce brought to China had a parallel in contemporary literature. Up to the nineteen-twenties all Chinese books were written in a style called 'wen yen', that is 'literary language'. This was a style quite un-related to spoken Chinese. It was extremely terse and included many words which had no spoken use at all. Although a very difficult medium, it was the vehicle of an immense literature whose earliest writings dated from the beginning of the first millennium B.C. Being a language of ideographs, little related to living speech, it had the great advantage of intelligibility throughout the ages.

All this changed in the 'twenties. Under the leadership of Hu Shih, a philosopher of distinction, the style of writing changed radically. The characters were retained but the idiom was that of everyday speech, in particular that of Peking. It was a democratization of writing. At the same time there was a flood of translation in the new style. The novels, politics, and economics of the West were translated in vast quantities. The literary change became a vehicle for the voice of young China. Many novels were written, their themes usually social injustice and the need for revolution, no longer the Confucian doctrine of filial piety, respect for superiors, and decorum. Marx, Darwin, and John Stuart Mill had taken the place of the Master. The young intellectuals demanded the emancipation of women—the end of foot-binding and polygamy and equal rights in education. The new writing in the idiom of 'clear speech' ('pai hua') was above all nationalist. It reflected a century of decline and humiliation and demanded the creation of a new China. The revolution of October 1911 had failed because of weak leadership, bad organization, and corruption among the revolutionaries themselves. Ten years later the clamour for change came from vastly greater numbers. And when Nationalism and Communism combined under the leadership of Sun Yat-sen the force of change could not be resisted.

Sun Yat-sen's political thought is contained in his *Autobiography,* his *Plans for National Reconstruction,* and above all his *San Min Chu I*—the *Three Principles of the People.* Long before the revolution of 1911, when he was travelling among the overseas Chinese in Hawaii and Singapore and when he addressed students in Europe and Japan, Sun had laid down the 'Three Principles' as the basis of the new Republic. It was not until 1924, however, that his fundamental thoughts were set forth in a clear and orderly manner. They were contained in sixteen lectures which he delivered in Canton when he was head of the Kuomintang and of the southern government.

The Three Principles are Min Tsu (People's Race or Tribe), Min Ch'uan (People's Rights), and Min Sheng (People's Livelihood) which can be roughly translated Nationalism, Democracy, and Livelihood. Together they represent a Western-style democratic republic with socialist leanings. His thinking was certainly not Communist for he explicitly rejected the notion of class struggle and the Marxist theory of surplus value. However, he believed that the State should control capital and land and that the initial period of the Republic should be one of dictatorship by his party, the Kuomintang. The period of 'tutelage' should continue until the revolution had removed all remnants of the old monarchy and had established conditions of peace and order when opposition parties might be permitted.

The principle of Nationalism may seem too obvious to need exposition but it was—and remains—the basic inspiration of all modern Chinese thinking. Sun Yat-sen was a pioneer of Asian nationalism. Until the Western powers came there was no need for nationalism. China was a world to herself, her culture was supreme. Her military defeat and political impotence in the nineteenth century, the collapse of her civilization and the humiliating insults she had to suffer, caused a deep and lasting sense of hurt which could only be remedied by a complete revolution inspired by fervent nationalism. This was the first and most viable of Sun's Three Principles. It is still the driving force of Mao Tse-tung's People's Republic.

In practical terms Sun's Nationalism included the denunciation of the 'unequal treaties' which, beginning with the Treaty of Nanking in 1842, had ceded pieces of China's territory to the Western powers, allowed foreign warships to patrol her rivers and exempted foreigners from Chinese law. Internally the people of China must be united, and not only the Chinese or Han people but also those races and minorities which were included in the Chinese Empire and its successor the Republic. These were the Tibetans, the Mongols, the Manchus, and the Mohammedans in the extreme west of China's territory. It is interesting to reflect that Sun included those non-Chinese peoples in his Nationalism, thinking of them as part of China's cultural domain. Sun saw

Chinese society as a 'rope of sand', millions of individuals with a common culture but without a sense of nationhood. By organizing the Hsing Chung Hui, the Tung Meng Hui, and finally the Kuomintang, Sun Yat-sen not only created the tools of revolution but also a sense of nationhood among his people.

The second Principle, Democracy, presents a system of government based largely on the British, French, and American patterns. Sun's ideas included the sovereignty of the people, universal suffrage and a national assembly elected by popular vote. The basic unit of government should be the 'hsien', the county or district which would send representatives to the provincial assembly as well as to the national assembly. The constitution of Sun's republic provided for a five-fold division of authority into the following categories: Legislative, Executive, Judicial, Control, and Examination. The last two were novel. Officials in the Control 'Yuan' (Department) were to act as a kind of censorship of the others on behalf of the people. The Examination Yuan was to act as a public service commission, testing all candidates for the civil service in a manner similar to the old imperial examinations.

Sun had the wisdom to realize that his ideas were not practicable immediately because of the ignorance of the peasants and workers. And so he envisaged a three-stage process, first a military dictatorship, then rule by one party only—the Kuomintang—and finally a liberal democracy in the Western style.

The third Principle, Min Sheng or people's livelihood is a statement of Sun's economic ideas. He envisaged a kind of socialism resembling that practised by the British Labour Party. Major industries would belong to the State. So should railways and all other communications. All capital should be 'controlled' to prevent the injustice of *laissez-faire*. He advocated land reform of a very radical kind. The peasant should own the land he cultivated. And when land value increased the increment should go in part to the State. Sun had been greatly impressed by the economic advance of America and Western Europe. The contrast of China's sordid poverty and illiteracy shocked and

D

roused him. But if his thoughts were radical they were certainly not Marxist or Communist.

Shanghai, the greatest of the 'concessions' created by the 'unequal treaties', was a useful refuge for political exiles and conspirators. Sun Yat-sen made it his home between bouts of politics and warfare in Canton. In cosmopolitan Shanghai he and his elegant wife Ching-ling worked on his *Autobiography* and *Plans for National Reconstruction*. Shanghai was rich, gay, and modern. The Sun house in the Avenue Joffre of the French Concession was handsome and comfortable. His library was choked with books on all manner of things but especially politics. There were many visitors—the Soong sisters, American journalists, fellow-revolutionaries, and old friends from his student days in Hong Kong.

Sun Yat-sen was now in his middle fifties and could have been excused for settling down in this congenial and luxurious city, devoting himself to writing and paternal advice to younger politicians in the field. But to a man of his disposition this was out of the question. Thinner, his face lined, and his moustache grey, Sun was as much the zealot as ever. If failure had tempered his optimism it had also hardened his resolve. Dressed in the neck-high grey-blue tunic (later to be the uniform of his Communist successors) Sun received visitors cordially but with a penetrating, unsmiling stare. He seldom if ever relaxed. Encouraged by his equally radical wife he used Shanghai, the metropolis of imperialism in China, as a base for new plans to re-build the broken republic.

He had two objectives; to smash the warlords, including General Wu P'ei-fu in Peking, and thus unite China under his Nationalist Party, the Kuomintang, and, secondly, to break the bonds of foreign domination. To do this he needed arms and money, and he had neither. In Canton he had had the support of the local warlord, Chen Chiung-ming, and he was to have his help again, but warlords were not good partners for idealists and visionaries. As for money, this was available—at a price—from the Western powers or Japan, but capitalist loans would increase China's subservience still more. All his life, like thousands of younger men from the universities of America and Europe, Sun had admired and sought to emulate the achievements of the West. Now came disillusionment. The Peace Treaty of 1919 had given Germany's concessions in China to Japan in spite of China's help to the Western Allies during the war. Western help and recognition went to Wu P'ei-fu in Peking, not to the Kuomintang. But the solution to Sun's dilemma lay at hand—an alliance with the Soviet Union. Sun had sent fraternal greetings to Lenin on the success of the 1917 Revolution. Now, some two years later the Soviet Union offered China a new relationship, free of all the privileges Tsarist Russia had gained in common with the other imperial powers. Sun did not decide immediately. He must first re-establish his government in Canton.

In another part of Shanghai's French Concession, not very far from the Sun house in the Avenue Joffre, a secret meeting was held in July 1921. It was attended by twelve Chinese and two foreigners. One of the Chinese was Mao Tse-tung, the son of a Hunanese peasant who had studied Marxism while a student at Peking University. The foreigners represented the Communist International. This was the First Congress of the Chinese Communist Party. It created the Party, drew up a provisional constitution, elected Mao as one of the two secretaries, and debated the tactics the Party should follow in the immediate future.

There were two alternatives—to fight the Kuomintang or to support it. The Chinese Communists knew that in the end they were basically opposed to Sun's type of revolution which they regarded as bourgeois. But the Chinese proletariat was not organized at all and the peasants were imprisoned in 'feudal' ideas. The Kuomintang, although not strong, was infinitely greater in numbers and appeal than their new party. It had an organization and its leader, Sun Yat-sen, was the symbol of the rising tide of Chinese nationalism. By the time of the First Congress Sun was back in Canton at the head of a new government. The Communist Party decided to co-operate with Sun.

Late in 1920 the warlord of Kwangtung had invited Sun Yat-sen to return to Canton to set up a government. For a warlord Chen was unusually progressive, at least for the time being. He promised allegiance to the Kuomintang and its leader. By the beginning of 1921 Sun had created a government with himself as President. Among his supporters were members of the first National Assembly which had been destroyed by Yuan Shih-kai. But the new government was entirely dependent on General Chen and his personal army for its existence let alone its hopes of expansion in a 'northern expedition' to make it the true government of China, not merely parts of the provinces of Kwangtung and Kwangsi.

Shortly after the conclusion of the First Congress of the Chinese Communist Party one of the two foreign delegates of the Communist International came to Canton for discussions with Sun. He was a Dutchman named Henriques Sneevliet, more commonly known by his assumed name of Maring. The talks were very friendly but inconclusive as no agreement was announced at their termination. This was surprising in view of Sun's earlier goodwill message to Lenin and a letter he had just sent to Chicherin, the Soviet Foreign Minister that same summer of 1921. In this he wrote:

'I would like to enter into personal contact with you and my friends in Moscow.... I am extremely interested in your work and particularly in the organization of your soviets, your army, and your educational system.'

Maring had come fresh from the Communist meeting in Shanghai and offered the co-operation of the new party. He pointed out that Sun could not succeed in conquering the warlords and uniting China for the Republic without a strong, mass party and a powerful army of his own. The Kuomintang members were mostly intellectuals who had been educated abroad or at the new schools. It had no contact with the ordinary people. As for an army, Sun was entirely dependent on General Chen, the warlord of the south. In spite of Sun's goodwill to Moscow and the cogent arguments of Maring it was more than

eighteen months before Sun accepted the co-operation of the
Chinese Communists. Why should he? The new party was still
negligible in numbers. His own party was extending its membership and was the focus of Chinese nationalism. Moreover, the
right wing of the Kuomintang saw danger in union with a
Marxist party and Sun himself may have been sceptical of Communist goodwill. The President of the Canton Government continued his efforts to consolidate and expand his authority in the
south without the aid of the Communists.

One hot morning in June 1922 Sun Yat-sen awoke to find his
villa surrounded by troops. The warlord of Kwangtung had
turned against him and staged a *coup d'état*. With his wife and a
few of his leading friends he escaped, made his way across the
rambling city and found safety on a warship in the river. He was
lucky to escape alive. With his government destroyed and the
Kuomintang members dispersed, Sun fled once more to the peace
of the French Concession in Shanghai. His second government
in Canton had lasted less than two years, destroyed by the General
who had called it into existence.

Although he was a refugee with neither a government nor an
army, Sun still had great power. Nationalist feeling among
students was rising. Demonstrations occurred in Shanghai against
foreigners and warlords. Sun had become the undoubted leader
of Chinese nationalism and it was merely a matter of time before he would return to the arena.

In August 1922 the Soviet Union sent Adolfe Joffe, one of
her ablest diplomats, to Peking to negotiate with Wu P'ei-fu on
the opening of relations between the two countries. Two years
earlier Moscow had declared her wish to treat China on terms
of equality, cancel all concessions and privileges, and renounce
her share of the Boxer Indemnity. These terms were again offered
and were accepted but difficulties arose over Russian control of
the Chinese Eastern Railway in Manchuria and on the sovereignty
of China over Outer Mongolia. These were academic matters for
General Wu's authority scarcely reached beyond the gates of
Peking. His government was recognized by the Powers although
almost the whole of China was dominated by warlords.

In the autumn Joffe exchanged the company of Wu P'ei-fu in Peking for that of Sun Yat-sen in Shanghai. The second negotiations were to prove very much more important than the first. Joffe succeeded where Maring had failed. He offered Soviet co-operation with the Kuomintang in order to achieve national unity and independence of the Western powers. At the same time Joffe proposed that the Kuomintang and the Chinese Communist Party should unite to achieve these objectives. Sun refused to accept this alliance. But he agreed that members of the Chinese Communist Party should be allowed to join the Kuomintang as individuals provided that they subscribed to the Three Principles of the People and obeyed the regulations of the Nationalist Party. Sun and Joffe also discussed the Chinese Eastern Railway and the spheres of influence of the two countries on their common frontier. Here, as with Wu P'ei-fu in Peking, the Russian encountered opposition. But on the matter of renouncing old Tsarist privileges there was obviously no difficulty.

After long discussions and hard bargaining, agreement between Sun Yat-sen and Joffe was reached in January 1923. It was an event of great importance. The Kuomintang was to co-operate with the Soviet Union and with the Chinese Communist Party. The two parties would not affiliate but Communists would be allowed to join the Nationalist Party as individuals. Russia would give up all her special rights in China and would supply Sun with arms and technical advice. Almost as valuable as the material aid was the simple fact of recognition and support from a great nation. Sun determined to return to his revolutionary base at Canton. A month after his discussion with Joffe, he had engaged the help of dissident military groups in Kwangtung and by the end of February had driven General Chen from Canton. Once again he established a government there. This time it was destined to triumph.

Sun Yat-sen and his Kuomintang government in Canton had turned left. Was the change dictated by expediency or conviction? Was it indeed a real change or merely a tactical manoeuvre to obtain Soviet arms and political support for the immediate objective of destroying the warlords and uniting China under the

Nationalists? The Chinese Communists, now admitted to the Kuomintang, had their own very clear motives—to join with Sun against the warlords and the foreign imperialists but also to influence the Kuomintang towards leftist policies and prevent it being dominated by 'reactionaries'. And when these objectives were achieved the Chinese Communist Party would proceed with its ultimate purpose, the proletarian revolution.

Sun Yat-sen may have been naïve in some of his actions in the past but can we say this of him in his decision to collaborate with the Soviet Union and the Chinese Communists? Perhaps the price of Russian arms and recognition—acceptance of support from the Chinese Communist Party—was worth paying. Or it may have been a genuine acceptance of the policy of the Soviet Union. After all, Joffe—and later Russian advisers—affirmed on several occasions that China was not ready for Communism. Their views were identical with Sun's on the immediate need to unify China under the Kuomintang and resist the imperialism of Japan and the Western powers.

In the summer of 1923 he sent his most promising military officer to Moscow to study the Red Army. This was Chiang Kai-shek, a clean-featured, sparely built, erect soldier in his mid-thirties. Chiang was impressed with what he saw. The U.S.S.R. was not yet six years old and already had an efficient government and a powerful army. In nearly a dozen years the Chinese Revolution (in which young Chiang had taken part) had achieved nothing. He returned to Canton after a three months tour determined to build a new Chinese army.

In the meantime Adolf Joffe had been replaced as Russia's envoy to China by L. M. Karakhan. Although in Peking negotiating with the government of Wu P'ei-fu, Karakhan sent a message of goodwill to Sun Yat-sen in Canton. Sun replied cordially and asked if the Russians could send him a political adviser. Early in October he arrived—Mikhail Borodin, officially a representative of the Rosta news agency but in fact a political adviser sent by the Communist International. In his fortieth year, Borodin had had considerable experience as a revolutionary in Russia, Mexico, and Britain. He had been imprisoned in Glasgow for his activities. He was a clever political theorist but, what was much more important for his mission to Canton, Borodin was an excellent organizer and had the right personality for the wilful Sun Yat-sen.

Borodin was given a comfortable villa in the eastern suburbs of Canton not far from Sun's residence. Sun was at first wary of his guest although his reception had been cordial. He closely interrogated the Russian about the Soviet Union and answered many questions about the situation in China. Both men spoke English fluently. In a few weeks it became clear that Borodin had won Sun's confidence. Soon more Russian advisers arrived in Canton, both military and political. Among them was a Vietnamese, a certain Nguyen Ai Quoc, better known as Ho Chi Minh, who was to become the President of the Communist state of North Vietnam some twenty years later. At the same time more Chinese Communists joined the Kuomintang, some of them occupying senior positions in the party. The Kuomintang was reorganized. Its membership had hitherto been confined to intellectuals, it had little contact with the peasants and workers. Throughout the two provinces which were controlled by the Canton Government—Kwangtung and Kwangsi—committees of the party were set up in villages and towns. Some of the most active organizers and propagandists were Communists. The right wing of the party began to complain that these agents were using the Kuomintang to spread Communism. But Sun rejected their overtures. Borodin, like Joffe before him, assured Sun that their objective was not Communism. What is more, it was clear to Sun and everybody else that the Nationalist Party was becoming for the first time an efficient, well-organized machine.

At the end of January 1924 the First Congress of the Kuomintang was held in Canton. Sun Yat-sen dominated the proceedings. He was elected head of the Kuomintang for life. His policy of co-operation with the Soviet Union and the Communists was ratified. His *Three Principles of the People* were proclaimed as the basic policies of the new China.

Sun Yat-sen was a good orator. The small figure in blue-grey tunic could hold and inspire an audience. Speaking slowly and quietly, his face defiant and proud, he commanded any audience. And he could play the demagogue, too, rousing his followers to fiery nationalism with loud and mounting denunciation of the imperialists and the 'unequal treaties'.

The conference was a triumph for two men—Sun Yat-sen and Mikhail Borodin. For the new, vital Kuomintang was largely of Borodin's making. He even drafted the party's new constitution which was then approved by Dr. Sun and the Congress.

In May 1924 the first Military Academy was opened at Whampoa, down the Pearl River estuary a short distance from Canton. General V. K. Blücher was the leader of a number of Soviet military advisers. The first commandant of the Academy was Chiang Kai-shek. Head of the political department of the Academy was Chou En-lai, a member of the Communist Party, later to become Prime Minister in Mao Tse-tung's People's Republic. Whampoa was an officer cadet school. It was the foundation of the Kuomintang army which was to sweep across China to victory in the spring of 1927.

In preparation for this 'northern expedition' Soviet arms and other military supplies began to arrive at Canton a few months after the opening of the Whampoa Academy. Sun had always planned such an expedition from his base in Canton. With a disciplined Kuomintang, Russian arms, and a modern army in training there was little doubt that he would soon be able to march north and defeat the warlords in central and north China. Perhaps in a year he would have enough strength to launch the expedition. The obvious course was to go on strengthening the Kuomintang army while consolidating his rule over the southern provinces. But Sun decided on another plan. He would go north to Peking himself and negotiate with the northern generals for unity under the Kuomintang. Borodin tried to dissuade him, but in vain. The warlord of Manchuria, General Chang Tso-lin, was threatening to seize Peking and made some show of accepting the Kuomintang Government. There seemed slender hope of winning over the generals without force but Sun was resolved on his mission and left for the north in November.

It was the last of his many journeys. He went to Shanghai where he held press conferences and was acclaimed by students and Kuomintang members. Still resolute and defiant, his face unsmiling, his eyes fixed in a penetrating stare as always, Dr. Sun was at the height of his fame and popularity. Now in his fifty-ninth year, he was not an old man but signs of exhaustion and pain could be seen in his face. He was a sick man.

In December, accompanied by his wife, Ching-ling, he sailed for Kobe. More meetings, speeches, and press interviews and then on to Tientsin in January 1925. Here, in the bitter northern winter, he was again welcomed and called upon to speak. Dressed now in a long, padded gown and wearing a Western-style hat, Sun was scarcely able to speak to his admiring followers. He felt the cold keenly after the mild southern winter and the pain was increasing. A special train took him to Peking. Preliminary discussions were held with the northern generals but Sun was too ill. He was taken to a missionary hospital and operated on by a German surgeon. He was suffering from cancer of the liver. His case was hopeless.

From the hospital he was taken to a friend's house. His wife, Ching-ling, and his son, Sun Fo, were summoned. Wang Ching-wei came north from Canton. The Father of the Republic was dying.

On the day before his death Sun Yat-sen signed a document which had been drafted by his colleagues when it was known that the end was near. This was his testament to the nation, his 'will', soon to be inscribed in public places throughout China and memorized by millions of students. Sun's 'will' reads as follows:

'For forty years I have devoted myself to the cause of the people's revolution with but one end in view, the elevation of China to a position of freedom and equality among the nations. My experience during these forty years has firmly convinced me that to attain this goal we must bring about a thorough awakening of our own people and ally ourselves in a common struggle with those peoples of the world who treat us on the basis of equality.

'The work of the Revolution is not yet done. Let all our comrades follow my *Plans for National Reconstruction, Fundamentals of National Reconstruction, The Three Principles of the People*, and the Manifesto issued by the First National Congress of our Party, and strive on earnestly for their consummation. Above all, our recent declaration in favour of the convocation of a National Convention and the abolition of unequal treaties should be carried into effect with the least possible delay. This is my heartfelt charge to you.

Sun Wen
March 11th, 1925.'

Sun also sent a message to Moscow:

'I leave behind me a party which, as I always hoped, will be allied with you in its historical task of liberating China and other suppressed peoples from the yoke of imperialism. My charge to the Kuomintang Party before all is that it shall continue to promote the course of the national revolutionary movement for the emancipation of China, which has been degraded by imperialism into a semi-colonial country. . . .'

The vocabulary as well as the sentiment was strongly Communist but, as if to right the balance, Dr. Sun insisted that he should have a Christian burial. He died on 12 March 1925.

There is no room here to bring the events of modern Chinese history up to the present but our account of the life of Sun Yat-sen would be incomplete if we omit all mention of what happened in the two decades following his death. For in that period his influence was at least as great as when he was alive. After his death he was almost deified. He became the Father of the Nation. His body was brought to Nanking and buried in a mausoleum grand enough for the tomb of an emperor. His portrait was everywhere, in the great buildings of Peking, in the new ministries at Nanking, and in the humblest homes and tea-houses. Religious devotion was paid to his memory. He embodied the new China.

After Sun's death Chiang Kai-shek took over in Canton. For two years the alliance with the Communists continued. By the autumn of 1926 Chiang had assembled enough strength to launch the northern expedition. Moving through the mountains of northern Kwangtung into Hunan the army was reinforced by peasant militia trained by Communist agents. Mao Tse-tung himself had been active in his native Hunan. The warlords in the path of the Kuomintang were routed. Hankow on the Yangtze was captured and in the spring of 1927 Nanking fell. Then quite suddenly, in April, Chiang struck at the Communists in his ranks. Many were executed. Others established a short-lived government in Hankow but they were soon dispersed and took to the hills. Borodin, Blücher, and the other Russians made a hurried departure overland from Hankow to the Soviet Union. The alliance with Moscow was denounced.

Chiang set up his new government at Nanking. A year or two later he had disposed of most of the northern warlords, taken Peking and renamed it Peiping. China was united for the first time since the revolution sixteen years before. It was a posthumous victory for Sun Yat-sen. But would he have fashioned it in this way? His alliance with the Soviet Union and the Chinese Communists, his speeches at the First National Congress of the Kuomintang, and the message to Moscow from his death-bed, all pointed to a very different Chinese unity from that imposed by his successor.

In the decade between the setting up of the Nanking government under Chiang Kai-shek and the Japanese attack in 1937 the image of Sun Yat-sen assumed god-like proportions, his Three Principles became scripture, his portrait an ikon. When the Communists again united with the Kuomintang in a common front against Japan, the alliance was specifically based on the *Three Principles of the People*. The alliance, an uneasy one throughout the war, collapsed after the Japanese defeat and civil war followed. The Red Army triumphed, Chiang and the Kuomintang fled to Taiwan and Mao proclaimed the People's Republic on 1 October 1949. Communist China did not reject Sun Yat-sen. Their leaders claim that they are his legitimate successors. So does the Kuomintang.

How great was Sun Yat-sen? Was he, in fact, a great man? Some would say he was much over-rated. He was a poor organizer, his judgement of men (Yuan Shih-kai, for example) was often ingenuous and faulty. His writings in politics are frequently superficial and make no contribution to political theory. But the quality of greatness need not lie only in these fields. Where Sun excelled was in being the voice and spirit of his time. He represented to humiliated and bewildered China a new light of hope. He was a visionary with complete faith in his vision of China. In a corrupt world he was free from reproach. His will was unbreakable. All his adult life he devoted 'to the cause of the people's revolution' and to 'a thorough awakening of the people'. His single-minded devotion to the re-establishment of the dignity of humiliated China won him the loyalty of all his people. Sun was Asia's first great nationalist. As his country's revolutionary patriot, Sun Yat-sen's position in modern history is assured. He led China into the twentieth century.

PRINCIPAL DATES

1866	Sun Yat-sen born at Choyhang village, Kwangtung province on 12 November.
1879	Sun goes to Honolulu to work in his brother's store.
1882	Withdrawn from Honolulu school and sent back to China.
1884	Admitted to Queen's College, Hong Kong in April.
1884–5	Sino-French War.
1886	Sun enters the Anglo-American Medical College at Canton.
1887	Enters Hong Kong Medical School.
1892	Qualifies as doctor and starts practice in Macao.
1893	Sun goes to practice in Canton, joins secret society.
1894	Outbreak of Sino-Japanese War over Korea in July. Sun abandons his medical practice and embarks on a political career.
1896	Sun travels in the United States and goes to England in September. Detained in Chinese Legation in London.
1898	Sun leaves London for Japan in July. The Hundred Days Reform by the Emperor Kwang Hsu. *Coup d'état* by the Empress Dowager.
1900	The Boxer Rebellion. Sun's Second Revolutionary Attempt.
1903–5	Sun on second world tour, Hawaii, the United States, and Europe.
1904–5	Russo-Japanese War, ending with Treaty of Portsmouth,

September 1905. Sun returns to Japan in July 1905. Organizes new revolutionary party, the T'ung Meng Hui.

1906   Death of Empress Dowager and Emperor Kwang Hsu on 15 November. P'u Yi, the last Manchu Emperor, enthroned.

1909–11   Sun on his third and last world tour.

1911   The October Tenth Revolution at Wuchang. Sun returns to Shanghai on 24 December, elected first Provisional President of China on 29 December.

1912   Inauguration of the Chinese Republic on 1 January. Abdication of the Emperor on 12 February. Sun resigns as President in favour of Yuan Shih-kai on 14 February. The Kuomintang inaugurated on 25 August.

1913   Yuan Shih-kai plans the destruction of the Republic. Sun flees to Japan. Civil war.

1914   Sun forms new party in Japan, the Chinese Revolutionary Party. He marries Soong Ching-ling in October.

1915–16   Yuan Shih-kai prepares to become Emperor. Dies on 6 June, 1916.

1917   Sun sets up military government in Canton.

1918–20   Sun unable to hold Canton, retires to Shanghai to write.

1920   Sun returns to Canton with support of local warlord.

1921   Founding of the Chinese Communist Party in July.

1922   Revolt in Canton; Sun again takes refuge in Shanghai.

1923   Sun has talks with Adolf Joffe in Shanghai. Beginning of the Kuomintang-Soviet and KMT–Chinese Communist alliance. Sun returns to Canton and sets up government. General Chiang Kai-shek goes to Russia. Mikhail Borodin sent to Canton in September to help reorganize Kuomintang.

1924   First National Congress of the Kuomintang held in January in Canton. The Whampoa Military Academy opened in June. Close Communist–Kuomintang co-operation. Soviet arms arrive at Canton in October. Sun goes to North to negotiate with Peking Government in December.

1925   Sun dies in Peking on 12 March.

FOR FURTHER READING

FOR the general history of China there is the authoritative *A Short History of the Chinese People* by L. Carrington Goodrich (Allen & Unwin). A most readable survey is *China, a Short Cultural History* by C. P. Fitzgerald (Cresset Press) and a good book dealing with the major achievements of Chinese culture is *The Legacy of China* edited by R. Dawson (O.U.P.).

The nineteenth century is dealt with by J. T. Pratt in *The Expansion of Europe in the Far East*, by G. E. Hudson in *The Far East in World Politics* (O.U.P.), by E. R. Hughes in *The Invasion of China by the Western World*, and by W. E. Soothill in *China and the West* (O.U.P.).

The period immediately before the Opium War is described in colourful manner by Austen Coates in his *Prelude to Hong Kong* (Routledge). Very readable accounts of the Opium War are given by Maurice Collis in his *Foreign Mud* (Faber), and by Arthur Waley in *The Opium War through Chinese Eyes* (Allen & Unwin). For the period dominated by Tzu Hsi there are *China under the Empress Dowager* by J. O. P. Bland (H. Vetch) and *Twilight in the Forbidden City* by Sir Reginald Johnston (Gollancz).

On Sun Yat-sen himself there is the book by Stephen Chen and Robert Payne—*Sun Yat-sen, a portrait* (John Day) which gives most of the facts but is uncritically eulogistic. Paul Linebarger has a number of books on Dr. Sun, including *The Political Doctrine of Sun Yat-sen* (John Hopkins Press) and *Sun Yat-sen and the Chinese Republic* (Century), but they tend to be too full of praise. Another life is Bernard Martin's *Strange Vigour, a biography of Sun Yat-sen* (Heinemann) written in a somewhat romantic vein.

Sun's own writings are not easy to come by in English except in libraries. They include his *Autobiography, Plans for National Reconstruction, Kidnapped in London*, and *Memoirs of a Chinese Revolutionary*. His *San Min Chu I* (the Three Principles of the People) has been published by the Chinese Cultural Society in Taiwan.

The period of the Kuomintang–Communist alliance is covered by general books on the modern period, such as *Chinese Communism* by Robert C. North (Weidenfeld and Nicolson), *Revolution in China* by C. P. Fitzgerald (Cresset Press), and *A History of Modern China* by K. S. Latourette (Penguin Books).

INDEX